# JUNIOR

# GIRL SCOUT ACTIVITY BOOK

Girl Scouts of the U.S.A.
420 Fifth Avenue
New York, N.Y. 10018

 GIRL SCOUTS OF THE U.S.A.

B. LaRae Orullian, *President*
Mary Rose Main, *National Executive Director*

Inquiries related to the *Junior Girl Scout Activity Book*
should be directed to Program, Girl Scouts of the U.S.A.,
420 Fifth Avenue, New York, N.Y. 10018.

*Project Coordinator:* Karen Unger Sparks
*Design:* Keithley and Associates, Inc.
*Illustrator:* Claire Sieffert

ISBN 0-88441-348-9

10 9 8 7 6 5 4 3 2 1

# CONTENTS

What are some of the best things about being a Junior Girl Scout? This book will help you find out! What do you think are some typical things that Junior Girl Scouts do in Girl Scouting? Well, actually, there is no one typical thing, because there is no one typical Junior Girl Scout! Every Girl Scout is special. You have unique talents and interests that you can explore further in the many activities in this book and in the other Girl Scout books. Each chapter in this book contains lots of activities on a particular theme. Many of the activities come from other Girl Scout books. Other activities are brand new. If you really enjoy one topic or one type of activity, you will discover that Girl Scouting has much more that you can do. You can also try something that you have never done before and discover new talents and new interests. You will certainly discover another reason why you are a special and unique person.

Girl Scouts share values and traditions with their sister Girl Scouts in the United States and in many other countries. Girl Scouts make the Girl Scout Promise and try to live by the Girl Scout Law. Have you memorized the Girl Scout Promise and Law?

## The Girl Scout Promise

On my honor, I will try:
To serve God and my country,
To help people at all times,
And to live by the Girl Scout Law.

Think of all the things you have done today. Think of what you are planning to do the rest of today and tomorrow. How will your actions show that you are a Girl Scout who believes in the Girl Scout Promise?

When you say you will do your best, you are making a commitment to try to live each of the ten parts of the Girl Scout Law every day. You are responsible to yourself and to others to become the best person that you can be. The people you meet in Girl Scouts, the friends that you make, and the

## The Girl Scout Law

I will do my best:
to be honest
to be fair
to help where I am needed
to be cheerful
to be friendly and considerate
to be a sister to every Girl Scout
to respect authority
to use resources wisely
to protect and improve the world around me
to show respect for myself and others
through my words and actions

experiences you have will all help you. There are millions of Girl Scouts, each one a very special person, who are living the Girl Scout Promise and Law every day with you and who are making a difference in their lives and in the lives of others.

Look through this book. Find something that interests you, that looks like fun to do, and get started. Share your achievements with your family and friends and always know that your sister Girl Scouts are very proud of all your accomplishments.

To learn more about Girl Scouting, look in these Girl Scout resources:

*Junior Girl Scout Handbook*, Chapter 1, "Welcome to Junior Girl Scouting," Chapter 5, "Leadership and Groups," Wider Opportunities badge

*Girl Scout Badges and Signs*, Chapter 1, "My Book of Badges and Signs," Girl Scouting Around the World badge, Girl Scouting in the U.S.A. badge

*Ceremonies in Girl Scouting*

*Outdoor Education in Girl Scouting*

*The Wide World of Girl Guiding and Girl Scouting*

*Trefoil Round the World*

*Games for Girl Scouts*, Chapter 8, "Girl Scout Lore and Skills"

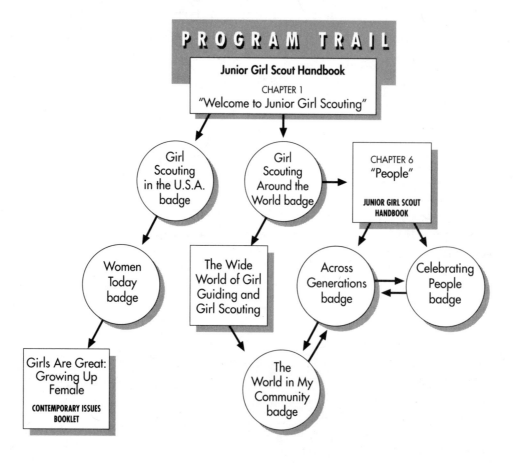

E ach day is the start of a whole new set of experiences. The more skills for living you have, the better able you will be to meet the opportunities and challenges that arise. Learning about yourself now can help you to figure out what kind of person you might want to be in the future. Read about three girls your age. How do their abilities and interests shape the goals that they have now?

## SANDRA'S STORY

Sandra is gifted in many ways. She consistently receives top grades in her class. She is also very popular. Her classmates recently elected her to be the president of their fifth-grade class. Sandra enjoys experimenting with the chemistry set she received for her birthday. She's an excellent swimmer and has joined her school's swim team. Sandra dreams of becoming a scientist someday, maybe even winning a Nobel Prize. Maybe she'll become a member of the United States Olympic swimming team or maybe study law or political science and run for office. Because she is so good at so many things, Sandra will have to make choices someday and that can be very hard to do.

## KATHERINE'S STORY

Eleven-year-old Katherine sings every chance she gets—on the way to school, in the shower, cleaning her room—but, always out of tune. She can practice all the time, but she will never be a good singer. Unfortunately, a singing career is what Katherine dreams of having. Katherine's music teacher at school doesn't have the heart to tell Katherine that she has no talent.

If only Katherine would realize that she should start dreaming of a different career. Perhaps she could develop her natural gracefulness and take dancing lessons. She gets excellent grades on all her writing assignments for school. Maybe she could become a journalist or writer. Katherine somehow has to realize that all the lessons in the world cannot make her a professional singer.

## MARIA'S STORY

At 12, Maria is the oldest of five children in her family. From the time Maria was seven, she was taking care of her younger brothers and sisters. Sometimes it was hard to be so responsible, but most of the time Maria thought it was fun. Maria has an extraordinary ability to get along with every child she meets. Children always run to Maria, tell her their secrets, ask her to be a part of their games. Maria has lots of friends, loves to play sports, and is well liked by her teachers and classmates. Maria wants to take education courses in college and become a kindergarten teacher. She understands who she is and what she is good at. Her special talents will probably allow her to fulfill her dream.

Think of the things that you do well. Think of the things that interest you. Write your own story here. Include your goals for the future.

_____

_____

_____

_____

_____

_____

_____

_____

_____

(Write your personal thoughts, feelings, daydreams, hopes, and stories in a journal or keep an audiotape record or scrapbook of mementos. Record your accomplishments so that you can compliment yourself on all the great things you have done.)

Activities on pages 3–4 are from the *Junior Girl Scout Handbook* and *Girl Scout Badges and Signs*.

To explore your talents further, follow the Program Trail for related activities.

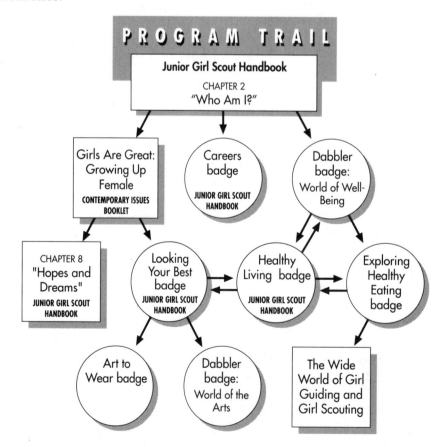

**Y**ou already know how to do hundreds of things and you'll learn hundreds more as you get older. You may not talk much about your skills and talents because you don't want others to think you're bragging, but this is your chance to brag. Complete these statements.

I am proud that I can _____

I am proud that I decided to _____

I am proud that I made my friends or family happy by _____

### *What's Important to You?*

Values are those things we hold dearest. Values are the things we believe are most important in our lives. Your values are shaped by many things—your family, your religious beliefs, your peers, and your own experiences. Your values may change as you grow older and are affected by new experiences. Try making some value judgments, decisions in which you think about what people, ideas, or things mean the most to you. As you answer each of these questions, think about what values you hold that led to your answer.

What living person do you most admire? _____

_____

Why? _____

_____

What do you like most about your best friend? _____

_____

Why? _____

_____

If you were given $100, how would you spend it? _____

_____

You can find out even more about your values by taking the quiz on the next page.

## Values Quiz

How important are each of these to you? Try to be very honest in your answers.

| | VERY IMPORTANT | IMPORTANT | NOT SO IMPORTANT | NOT IMPORTANT |
|---|---|---|---|---|
| Being well-liked | | | | |
| Being a class leader | | | | |
| Participating regularly in religious services | | | | |
| Having very stylish clothes | | | | |
| Getting good grades in school | | | | |
| Doing things with your family | | | | |
| Doing exciting things | | | | |
| Being famous someday | | | | |
| Having children someday | | | | |
| Having one or two best friends | | | | |
| Learning new things | | | | |
| Earning a lot of money | | | | |

By looking at the items that you checked as "Very Important," you will get an idea of what things mean the most to you.

Activities on pages 5–6 are from the *Junior Girl Scout Handbook*.

To do other activities on values, follow the Program Trail.

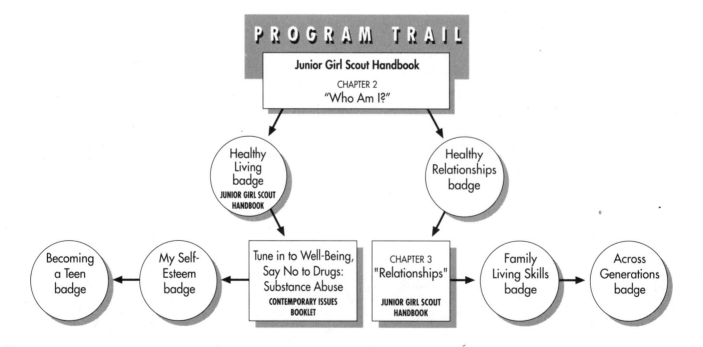

# MONEY MANAGEMENT

**D**o you get an allowance? Have you ever earned money babysitting or doing chores for someone? How would you spend money that you get as a gift? At one time or another, you have probably had some money of your own. You had to make some decisions on how to spend it. Did you save it, spend it, or donate it to a special cause? Making decisions about money is not always easy, but you will have to make many more of these kinds of decisions as you grow older.

## LAUREN'S MONEY

Lauren's neighbor, Mrs. Costa, was about to start a new job and needed someone to walk her two dogs every weekday morning and afternoon. She offered Lauren the job. Lauren couldn't believe her luck. The $15 she would get each week sounded terrific. Lauren said yes. The latest tape, the sneakers she had seen at the mall, maybe save for her own CD player.... Lauren couldn't stop thinking of all the things she could buy with this money. Suddenly, her mother interrupted her daydreams. "Lauren, this is a good time for you to open a savings account and start saving money for college. You know that it will be very expensive and we do expect you to contribute." Lauren was crushed! Her spending money had disappeared before she had even earned it!

What are Lauren's choices? Think of your own ending to Lauren's situation.

Lauren was upset for a while, but finally spoke with her mother. Her mother agreed to let Lauren keep half of her money and save the other half for college.

How do you spend your money? Keep track of your personal budget for a month. Write down the money you receive, spend, and save. Where does your money go? How much can you save?

How much does it cost to live in your area? What kind of lifestyle do you expect to have when you get older? Would you rather live in a house or an apartment? Do you need a car or could you use public transportation? How much money would you spend on food? Would you eat out or cook your meals? How much would you spend on clothing? travel? insurance? entertainment? What other expenses would you have?

Get a copy of your local newspaper. Find some advertisements for the types of jobs you would like to have. What salaries do these jobs offer? How much is each salary per month? Subtract 20 percent (1/5) of this salary for taxes. The new figure is your net salary—what you take home. Now look in the ads for the type of apartment you would like to have, or find out how much a house would cost and how much you would need to pay each month for a mortgage (ask an adult to help you). Find out how much a car and car insurance or public transportation would cost. Look up food prices. Try completing the monthly budget below. How much money do you need to make each month to live the way you would like to live? What kinds of jobs would pay you that amount of money? What would you need to do in order to get those kinds of jobs?

| MONTHLY BUDGET | |
| --- | --- |
| Monthly salary | |
| Rent or mortgage payment | |
| Car or transportation | |
| Food | |
| Clothing | |
| Entertainment | |
| Savings | |
| Health care | |
| Miscellaneous | |
| TOTAL: | |

Activities on pages 7–8 are from the *Junior Girl Scout Handbook* and *Girl Scout Badges and Signs*.

To do more activities on money management, follow the Program Trail.

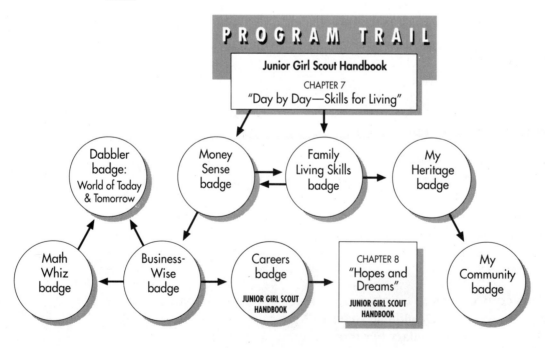

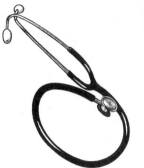

**Y**our values, your talents, and your interests will all influence your future plans. Many women today will work outside the home. Some women will decide not to have children. Many will balance children and family responsibilities with work responsibilities. Women who would prefer to stay at home with their children may decide or need to work as their children grow up. Women have more job opportunities today than ever before. The hard part is deciding what you would like to do. Your abilities and interests can guide you, as can the kind of life you would like to have. What is important to you? Some careers are fun and creative, but do not pay much money. Some pay a lot of money, but may be very difficult. Some careers combine both qualities. The more information you have about the many different types of jobs that exist, the better able you will be to start thinking about your future.

Match the job to the skills/interests/training needed to do it. (See next page for answers.)

A   Veterinarian

B   Fashion designer

C   Certified public accountant

D   Registered nurse

E   Elementary school teacher

F   Auto mechanic

G   Musician

H   Park ranger

I   Astronaut

J   Police officer

**1** Four years of college/major in accounting/pass a national exam/internship  _____

**2** High school education/pass a written exam and physical exam/special training  _____

**3** Four years of college with a major in nursing or hospital-based program  _____

**4** Three or four years of training at a college or design school/apprenticeship  _____

**5** Four years of college/major in forestry or environmental science/internship  _____

**6** Six or more years of college/two years of special training/experience with high-performance aircraft or special experience in the sciences, mathematics, or engineering  _____

**7** On-the-job training or vocational school training/ apprenticeship  _____

**8** Four years of college with major in education/ internship/state certification  _____

**9** Four years of college in science and four years at a school of veterinary medicine  _____

**10** Extensive study of one or more instruments/ degree from a music school or four years of college with a major in music  _____

Find out more about a job that interests you.

Job: _____

Education needed to do this job: _____

_____

Special training/abilities _____

_____

Role models are people who are doing the kinds of jobs which interest you. Role models are important sources of inspiration and information. You can read about role models in books and magazines. You might hear about some on TV. You could try interviewing one. Ask why she chose her career, what she likes and doesn't like, or what her average day is like. If you can get permission, try "shadowing" her for one day. Find out if she is a parent. If she is, how does she manage her time between family and work?

Activities on pages 9–10 are from the *Junior Girl Scout Handbook*, *From Dreams to Reality: Career Cards*, and *Preventing Teenage Pregnancy: Decisions for Your Life* Contemporary Issues booklet.

For other activities on careers and role models, follow the Program Trail.

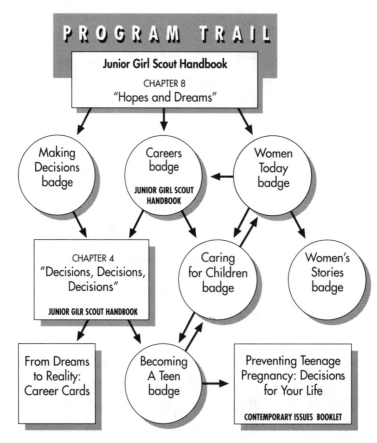

**ANSWER KEY:** A–9; B–4; C–1; D–3; E–8; F–7; G–10; H–5; I–6; J–2

# PLANNING TO REACH A GOAL

**W**hat are some things you want to accomplish today? What about next week? Next year? Things that you want to accomplish are your goals. People set goals all the time. Some are easy, such as "I'll wash these dishes before I go to bed," and some are hard, such as "I want to graduate from medical school before the age of 16!" What is easy and what is hard are different for each person. Your goals can also change. What you set as a goal for your future now may change when you are older. One sure thing is that in order to reach any goal you will need to plan. Many businesses make action plans. They write down the different steps they will need to complete in order to reach their goals and they set a time for each step to be completed. This type of action planning is very useful for you to use to reach your own personal goals.

*My Personal Action Plan*

My goal: _____

_____

Steps I will need to reach my goal: _____

_____

_____

_____

_____

Planned date of completion for each step: _____

_____

_____

_____

_____

_____

People who can help me reach my goal: _____

_____

_____

_____

_____

_____

How they can help me: _____

_____

_____

_____

On the date you thought your goal would be reached, do this checklist.

| | | YES | NO |
|---|---|---|---|
| **1** | My goal has been reached. If you answered yes, go to question number 6. | ☐ | ☐ |
| **2** | I am no longer interested in this goal. | ☐ | ☐ |
| **3** | I did not put enough effort into reaching this goal. | ☐ | ☐ |
| **4** | I need to change the steps and try again. | ☐ | ☐ |
| **5** | I am still working on my goal. | ☐ | ☐ |
| **6** | I am happy with my effort to reach my goal. | ☐ | ☐ |

(Ask your friends what their hopes and dreams are for the future. What kinds of careers interest them? How will they use their abilities and interests?)

The activities on pages 11–12 are from the *Junior Girl Scout Handbook* and *Girls are Great: Growing Up Female* Contemporary Issues booklet.

To find more activities on goal-setting, follow the Program Trail.

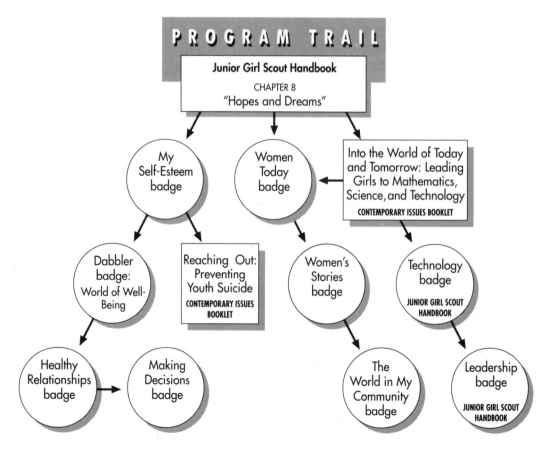

Everyone's world is filled with people. Think of all the people you interact with every day. Some people you meet once and never see again. Some people, like your family, friends, classmates, teachers, and Girl Scout leader, are close to you. You have a relationship with these people. Each relationship is unique, but all relationships involve sharing, talking, and spending time together. Some relationships seem to require very little effort. Are there some people with whom you never seem to disagree or get angry? Other relationships, though, may require work to stay healthy.

Listening to others is a good way to keep relationships strong. What does she really mean? Why is she saying that? People can become so busy thinking about what they want to say next that they don't really hear what the other person is saying. Here are some tips for listening well:

- Look at the person who is talking.
- Try not to think about other things. Concentrate on what the other person is saying.
- Try not to interrupt or think about what you will answer.

When the person is finished speaking, try repeating or restating what you heard. You can start by saying, "Did you say that . . . ?" or "In other words . . ." or "It sounds like you said . . ." or whatever feels comfortable to you.

Try creating conversations for the situations below, using the ways to listen described above.

- Your classmate tells you that she heard your best friend say something bad about you. Just then you see your best friend walking toward you.
- Your friend invites you to go shopping on Saturday. Your mother has asked you to watch your younger brother. You really want to go with your friend.
- You are responsible for getting your younger sister ready for school in the morning. This has made you late for class every day this week. Finally, the teacher takes you aside and asks you why you've been late.
- You promise to help your friend study for a quiz tomorrow. Your father comes home and suggests that the family go out to a movie.

When you listen well, you try to empathize with other people—understand what they are feeling and thinking. Think of a favorite fairy tale, folk tale, or movie plot. Try to rethink the story from the "villainess's" point of view. For example, how would the story of Goldilocks be different if one of the bears told the story today?

When this little blonde girl moved down the street, we didn't think anything of it. We get along with all our neighbors in this part of the woods. We look after their cubs; they look after ours. If someone goes on vacation, we keep an eye on her den. So, when we took our annual trip to visit the relatives in Yellowstone, we weren't worried at all—just looking forward to communing with nature. Well, you can imagine how upset we were when we got back to find the whole den turned upside down. First, someone had been moving all the chairs around. We thought it was the ghost of Winnie the Pooh! Then, we saw someone had been in the kitchen, and actually had the nerve to eat our porridge. We were scared to death to go upstairs, but when we remembered that our winter's supply of honey was hidden in the bedroom closet, we just had to look . . . *(Try writing your own ending to this story on a separate page.)*

Try creating a play, skit, rap song, comedy routine, cartoon, or other way to retell your favorite story.

The activities on pages 13–14 are from the *Junior Girl Scout Handbook* and *Girl Scout Badges and Signs*.

For other activities on listening, follow the Program Trail.

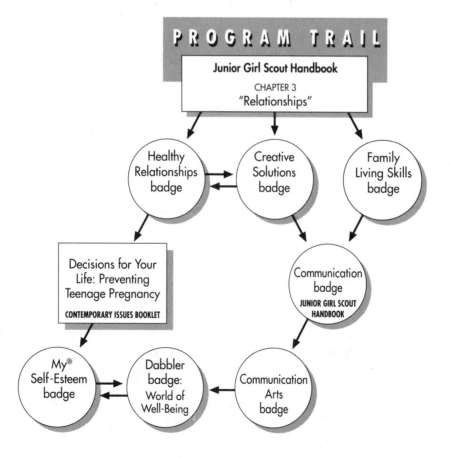

PROGRAM TRAIL

Junior Girl Scout Handbook
CHAPTER 3
"Relationships"

Healthy Relationships badge

Creative Solutions badge

Family Living Skills badge

Decisions for Your Life: Preventing Teenage Pregnancy
CONTEMPORARY ISSUES BOOKLET

Communication badge
JUNIOR GIRL SCOUT HANDBOOK

My Self-Esteem badge

Dabbler badge: World of Well-Being

Communication Arts badge

**A** family is made up of the people who care for and support you. Members of your family can be mother, father, sisters, brothers, grandparents, great-grandparents, stepparents and stepbrothers and stepsisters, foster parents, guardians, aunts, uncles, or cousins. They may live with you, nearby, or far away. What makes a family special? A family provides love, security, food, clothing, shelter, support, safety, and a sense of being important.

A "coat of arms" was used in medieval times to represent the values and strengths of a family. Try designing one for your family in the space below. You may include symbols of your family's values, things important to your family, the activities that your family enjoys, or anything that makes your family unique and special. Try to think of a family motto to go along with your coat of arms.

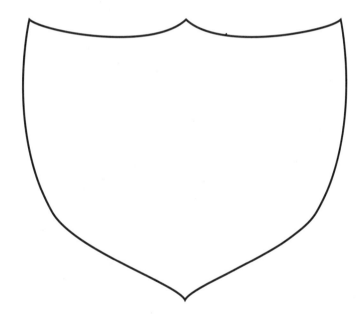

Collect or make pictures of the important events that have happened in the history of your family. Make a timeline, mobile, drama, or display that shows these events.

### What Is a "Typical" Family?

Watch several television programs or movies or read several books or stories about families. Look for the responsibilities each family member has, the way decisions are made, how problems are solved, what conversations between adults and children are like, and the ways families share and help each other. Compare these families to families that you know. How do the fictional families compare to the real families? How are they the same and how are they different?

## What Is a Parent?

What are a parent's responsibilities? Interview several parents. Ask them how their lives changed when they had children. Try to find out how much having children costs. With a group of friends, take turns imagining that you are a parent. Act out what you would do if your child:

- Wouldn't stop crying.
- Made the track team.
- Got a low grade in reading on her report card.
- Came home late from school.
- Made dinner for the family one night.
- Was accused of shoplifting.
- Yelled at her younger sister.
- Won a good citizenship award from the town council.

The activities on pages 15–16 are from the *Junior Girl Scout Handbook*, *Girl Scout Badges and Signs*, and *Caring and Coping: Facing Family Crises* Contemporary Issues booklet.

For other activities on families, follow the Program Trail.

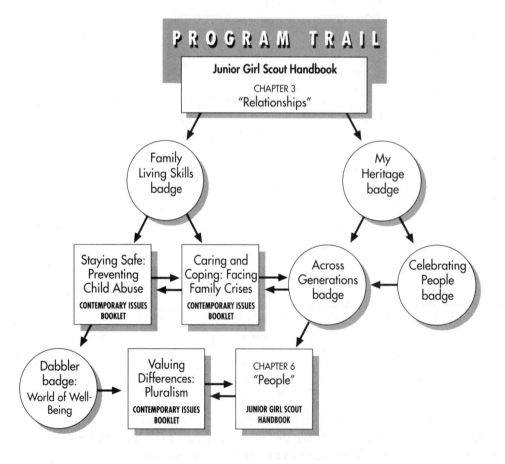

**PROGRAM TRAIL**

Junior Girl Scout Handbook
CHAPTER 3
"Relationships"

Family Living Skills badge

My Heritage badge

Staying Safe: Preventing Child Abuse
CONTEMPORARY ISSUES BOOKLET

Caring and Coping: Facing Family Crises
CONTEMPORARY ISSUES BOOKLET

Across Generations badge

Celebrating People badge

Dabbler badge: World of Well-Being

Valuing Differences: Pluralism
CONTEMPORARY ISSUES BOOKLET

CHAPTER 6 "People"
JUNIOR GIRL SCOUT HANDBOOK

friend is an important person.

**FRIENDS:**
care about each other.
are there for each other.
can be trusted.
can keep secrets.
believe in each other.
respect each other's ideas and values.
enjoy being together.

Friendship depends a lot upon you. What kind of friend are you? Answer each statement "yes" or "no."

|  | YES | NO |
|---|---|---|
| I listen carefully to my friend when she talks about something important to her. | ☐ | ☐ |
| I might be upset with my friend but I still speak to her. | ☐ | ☐ |
| It doesn't bother me if my friend is sometimes too busy to see me. | ☐ | ☐ |
| I let my friend know what I like about her. | ☐ | ☐ |
| We both make decisions on how to spend our time together. | ☐ | ☐ |
| My friend can trust me with her secrets. | ☐ | ☐ |
| I do not try to make my friend just like me. | ☐ | ☐ |
| My friend and I like to do things together. | ☐ | ☐ |

Count how many times you answered "yes." If your score is

| 7 or 8 | You are a super friend! |
|---|---|
| 5 or 6 | You are a good friend. |
| 4 | You need to work a little harder on being a friend. |
| 3 or below | Help! Start being a good friend before it is too late—begin with these eight steps. |

Levels of friendship differ. You will not be equally close to everyone. Friendships also can change. You may stay friends with someone throughout your life, or friendships may end and new friendships start as you grow and change. You may not do or talk about the same things with all your friends, and different friends may see different parts of your personality. For each statement, write down the name of a friend who comes to mind.

If I needed help with my schoolwork, I would ask _____.

If I were in a bad mood, I know I would feel better if I spent time with _____.

If I had a big secret, I know I could trust _____.

If I wanted to buy some new clothes, I would bring _____.

If I were having a party, the first person I would invite would be _____.

Are there many different names? Do you think the names you have written here will be different a year from now?

The activities on pages 17–18 are from the *Junior Girl Scout Handbook*.

For more activities on friendship, follow the Program Trail.

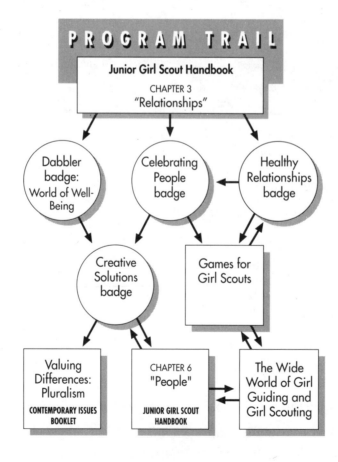

Whenever you are a part of a group, even just you and one other friend or family member, you are using your social skills to get along with other people, to be well-liked, to try to convince others to see things your way or to agree with you, to share information that you have, or even to get support or help from others. But, everyone is different. You and your friends and members of your family have different ideas and different ways of doing things and may even have different values and interests. These differences make life interesting and creative and fun, but they can also sometimes cause problems. These types of problems are called conflicts. A conflict happens when two or more people (friends, family, neighbors), or two or more groups (schools, countries), want the same thing or cannot agree. Conflicts can also happen inside yourself when you are not sure what you want.

### *Some Examples of Conflicts*

Between two friends _____

Between a parent and a child _____

Between two neighbors _____

Between two countries _____

How could these conflicts be solved? The best solution when resolving a conflict is for everyone to "win." If only one person wins, then the other person will be unhappy. If no one wins, two people will be unhappy. What steps can we use to make two people happy?

1. State the problem.
2. Each person states the other person's point of view.
3. Brainstorm some possible solutions.
4. Agree on one.

These steps may not work for every conflict, but they will resolve most. Conflicts can often get worse or blow up because of the way people communicate. What happens when you get angry? Do you listen? Do you say hurtful things? Do you want to win—any way you can? Using the word "you" to start a sentence in an argument can often make things worse—"You make me so angry," "You always get your way"—because the other person will quickly defend herself, "No, I don't," and the conflict gets bigger and longer. Starting sentences with "I" can make a big difference. When you start sentences with "I," you are speaking for yourself. Instead of saying, "You make me so mad when you borrow my stuff without asking," you could say, "I like knowing where my things are. I feel upset when I want to use something and can't find it. What can we work out?" Feel

**19**

the difference. No one is being accused of anything; no one's feelings are hurt; no one gets defensive; and the conflict (borrowing things without asking) can be resolved quickly. Using the four steps above and using statements that begin with "I," try resolving the conflicts below. You might want to practice with a friend.

- Your teacher accuses you of talking, but it was the person behind you.
- You share a room with your younger sister. She is very messy and you are neat.
- A girl whom you think is popular asks if you would like to smoke a cigarette. You know smoking is bad for you.
- You have made some new friends this year. A girl with whom you were friendly last year invites you over to spend the night, but you are not sure yet what your new friends are doing this weekend.
- An older girl dares you in front of a group to steal a lipstick from the drugstore. She calls you a baby and asks if you are afraid.
- Many of your girlfriends have pierced ears and are wearing hoop earrings to school. Your mom will not let you get your ears pierced.

Think of a situation that happened to you. How did you resolve it at the time? Would you resolve it differently now?

The activities on pages 19–20 are from *Girl Scout Badges and Signs*.

For more activities on getting along with others, follow the Program Trail.

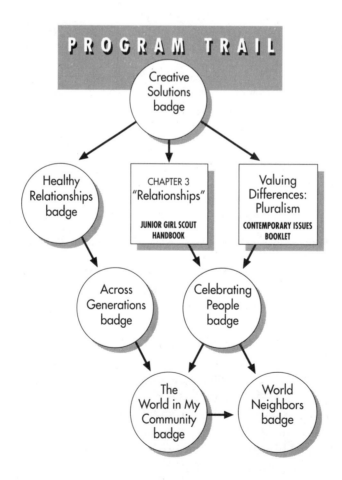

# COOPERATIVE GAMES AND PUZZLES

**T**ry your cooperative skills on these games and puzzles!

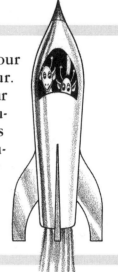

Imagine the following situation:

You are an Ardavanian ruler from the Planet Ardavania. Your planet gets a lot of sun and is very warm, but has very little water. This makes it difficult to grow enough food for everyone. Nearby, the Planet Frazar has very dim sunlight, so most of the planet, which is three-fourths water, is covered by ice. The Frazarians are envious of your sunlight and warmth. They have sent you a message to surrender your planet. Their spaceships will enter your atmosphere in one hour. With a group, or on your own, think of as many solutions as you can to this problem. Would your solutions be different if Frazar had no water? How can you reach a solution in which your planet and Frazar both win?

With a group, try the following:

■ Create a giant machine. Each member of the group acts as a part of the machine—a wheel, a gear, a knob, etc. See how well the group can work together.

■ Using drinking straws or toothpicks, try to make a group structure or creation. Each member of the group should help build it and decide what it will be.

■ Sit in a circle. Start with a wound ball of yarn. Toss it to one of the members of the circle. That person begins a story. She then tosses the yarn to another member of the circle, who continues the story. The group members keep tossing the yarn, adding to the story until the yarn is unwound.

■ Try cooperative musical chairs. One chair is removed every time the music stops, but everyone must balance on the chairs that are left. The game ends when there is only one chair left and everyone is somehow sitting on it.

■ Make a human knot. Everyone stands in a circle, places their hands in the center, and takes hold of the hands of two people other than those standing next to her. Then try to untie the knot without releasing any hands!

■ Try resting without a chair! Stand in a circle, each person facing the back of the person in front of her. Everyone takes a side step toward the center of the circle so that everyone is standing close together. When the circle is tight, the leader says, "Lap sit!" and everyone carefully sits on the lap of the person behind her.

Try inventing your own cooperative game here!

The activities on pages 21–22 are from *Games for Girl Scouts* and *Girl Scout Badges and Signs*.

For other activities on cooperative games, follow the Program Trail.

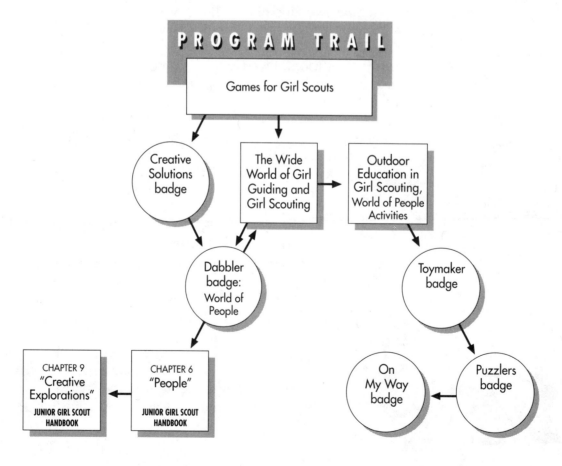

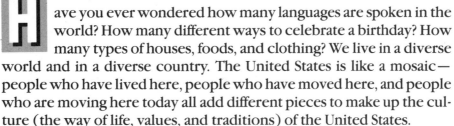

# CHAPTER 3
# MANY DIFFERENT KINDS OF PEOPLE

Have you ever wondered how many languages are spoken in the world? How many different ways to celebrate a birthday? How many types of houses, foods, and clothing? We live in a diverse world and in a diverse country. The United States is like a mosaic—people who have lived here, people who have moved here, and people who are moving here today all add different pieces to make up the culture (the way of life, values, and traditions) of the United States.

What is your cultural heritage? Some people identify strongly with one cultural or ethnic group; some people with two or more groups. Some people may identify with the place they grew up or with many different cultures. People who share the same cultural background may also be very different; they may have different values, traditions, and even languages.

Find a way to celebrate your heritage. What have you inherited that makes you the unique and special person that you are? How can you show that you are proud of your heritage? Write down some ideas here.

_____

_____

_____

_____

Ask older people in your family or older people who share your cultural background to tell you about their lives, interesting events, or special stories they could share. Can you discover more about your heritage?

Finding out about your family's history can be lots of fun. Interview relatives who know your family story. Make an audio- or videotape of your interview. Include a scrapbook of special mementos, photographs, and documents. Here are some questions you may want to ask.

**1** What were your childhood and teen years like (school, hobbies, playtime)?

**2** Do you remember any stories your parents or grandparents told about their childhood or family history?

**3** What is your favorite memory?

**4** Do you remember an event that had special importance for you?

**5** Do you remember any special customs or traditions?

*Family Recipes:* Many families share a special way of cooking food. Often treasured recipes are passed along from parents to children. Many of these recipes appear at family celebrations. Do you have a special family recipe? If you don't, why not invent a new tradition for your family?

MY RECIPE _____ SERVINGS _____

INGREDIENTS: _____

_____

_____

DIRECTIONS: _____

_____

_____

The activities on pages 23–24 are from the *Junior Girl Scout Handbook*, *Girl Scout Badges and Signs*, and *Girl Scout Leader* magazine (Spring 1989).

For more activities on exploring one's heritage, follow the Program Trail.

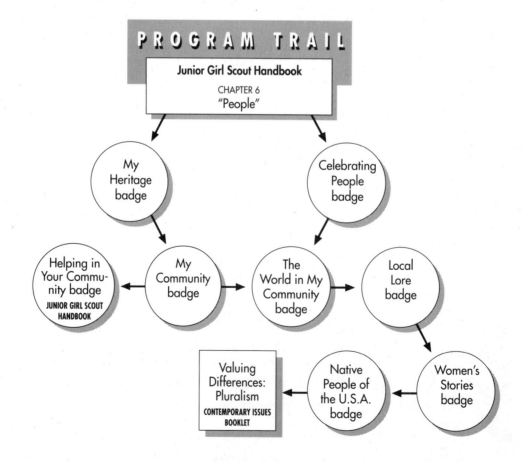

PROGRAM TRAIL

Junior Girl Scout Handbook
CHAPTER 6
"People"

My Heritage badge

Celebrating People badge

Helping in Your Community badge
JUNIOR GIRL SCOUT HANDBOOK

My Community badge

The World in My Community badge

Local Lore badge

Valuing Differences: Pluralism
CONTEMPORARY ISSUES BOOKLET

Native People of the U.S.A. badge

Women's Stories badge

**A** community consists of all the people who live in one geographic area. A community also means people who share more than just a place to live. Community implies a group of people who care for each other and who work together to make the place that they live better. The people who live in a community can have diverse backgrounds, interests, traditions, and customs, but they all share a common home.

What can you discover about the diversity of the community? Draw a map of your community (or neighborhood). On your map, highlight the contributions of people from a variety of racial and ethnic backgrounds, either from the past or the present. Some things you might look for are statues, memorials, and monuments, street names, park names, restaurants, shops, businesses, names of geographic features, historic houses and buildings, names of trails, rivers, specific neighborhoods, agriculture, etc. A local phone book could be helpful, as could your library or historical society.

Interview older family members or neighbors. How were they affected by these twentieth-century events: the Great Depression, World War II, the Civil Rights Movement, the Vietnam War, the Women's Movement? What events are happening now that you think may influence the future?

A person with a disability is "unable" to do certain things. She may have trouble hearing, seeing, talking, learning, or walking or have a special health problem like epilepsy or a heart condition. People with disabilities are as diverse as people without disabilities. Every person has many abilities. Every person has some things that she can do better than others.

Survey your community or school to find out how easy or hard it is for people with disabilities to get around. Interview a friend, classmate, or someone else you know with a disability to get her perspective.

The activities on pages 25–26 are from the *Junior Girl Scout Handbook* and *Girl Scout Badges and Signs*.

For more activities on your community, follow the Program Trail.

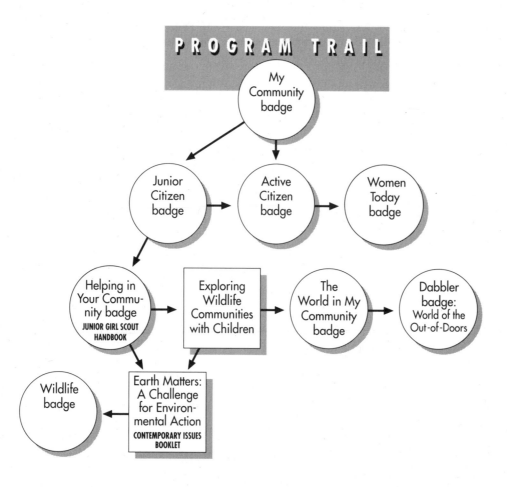

PROGRAM TRAIL

My Community badge

Junior Citizen badge

Active Citizen badge

Women Today badge

Helping in Your Community badge
JUNIOR GIRL SCOUT HANDBOOK

Exploring Wildlife Communities with Children

The World in My Community badge

Dabbler badge: World of the Out-of-Doors

Wildlife badge

Earth Matters: A Challenge for Environmental Action
CONTEMPORARY ISSUES BOOKLET

Prejudice occurs when someone fears or dislikes a person because of her racial, ethnic, cultural, or religious background or because she is different in some way. Prejudiced people often do not really know another person who is different. They also usually have low self-esteem, which is why they are so afraid of people who are different. People who are prejudiced may stereotype a particular group of people, that is, they believe all people who belong to one group are the same or behave in the same way.

Being prejudiced stops you from enjoying the interesting and exciting things that come from diversity. It also makes your mind and feelings stop growing. When your mind stays small and your heart shrivels, you can't be as happy and as smart as you could have been. You never really reach your potential.

Imagine that you are from another part of the universe and you are circling Planet Earth in your spaceship. You have never visited Planet Earth before and you must make a report to your superiors about this planet. How would you answer these questions in your report?

1. What are the common characteristics of the inhabitants of this planet?

2. What activities do they enjoy?

3. What are their beliefs and what things are important to them?

4. What do they need in order to survive?

5. How do the inhabitants treat each other and how do they treat their planet?

Try writing your report here.

_____

_____

_____

_____

_____

_____

_____

Share your answers with others. Try creating a skit, cartoon strip, story, fable, or song about your discoveries concerning Planet Earth.

What is a clique? How do cliques develop? How does it feel to be part of a clique—outside of a clique? What kind of ending can you give the following story?

Meggie woke up one hour before the alarm clock would ring and wished it were Saturday, not Friday. "I really do feel sick," she thought. "My stomach hurts. I feel achy and tired and I really want to stay home." The room was still dark, but Meggie could see the events of last week—just like a movie—appear in front of her. Stacey had been her closest friend since they were little kids. But, Stacey's dad had gotten a promotion. Stacey now had a built-in pool. When they were building it, she and Meggie couldn't stop laughing about all the cute boys they would invite to these great pool parties they would have. But now, this past week, Stacey had been sitting at a lunch table with a different group. There was never an extra seat left for Meggie. Stacey wouldn't look up when Meggie entered the cafeteria, and one day, two of the girls at the table pointed to her as they whispered something to Stacey and the whole table started to laugh. After school and during breaks, Stacey seemed to just disappear, and when Meggie tried to call her, her Mom said that Stacey wasn't home. Her Mom sounded sad somehow. Meggie thought, "I've never felt so lonely."

My ending: _____

_____

_____

The activities on pages 27–28 are from *Girl Scout Badges and Signs* and *Valuing Differences: Pluralism* Contemporary Issues booklet.

For more activities on getting along with others, follow the Program Trail.

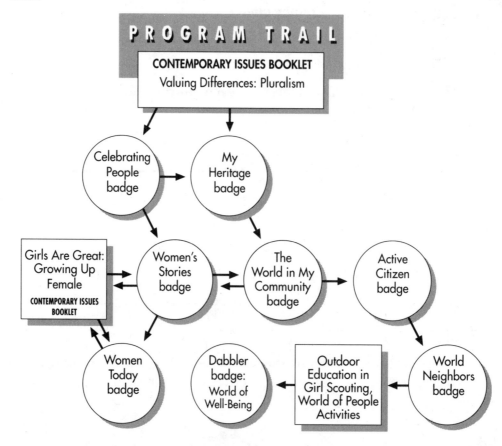

PROGRAM TRAIL

CONTEMPORARY ISSUES BOOKLET
Valuing Differences: Pluralism

Celebrating People badge

My Heritage badge

Girls Are Great: Growing Up Female
CONTEMPORARY ISSUES BOOKLET

Women's Stories badge

The World in My Community badge

Active Citizen badge

Women Today badge

Dabbler badge: World of Well-Being

Outdoor Education in Girl Scouting, World of People Activities

World Neighbors badge

**S**ome people call the earth a "global village." How large a community is a village? What does "global" mean? People who live in countries that are very far apart geographically share news events, fashions, and culture through television and radio. Countries depend on each other by importing and exporting products, information, and ideas. No country can make all the products its people want or grow all the food and materials its people need.

Try a global village hunt. Look around your home, your school, and your supermarket. Read labels. Where were these products grown or made? How many countries can you find? With a group, see who can find the most.

Hungry people do not live only in poorer countries. Wealthy countries, including the United States, have hungry people, too. Find out about what is being done to help people who are hungry. Interview your school cafeteria officials to find out how much food is wasted each week. Or, keep track of how much food your family wastes in one week. What can you do to waste less food? Does your community have a food bank or other plan to help hungry people? Think of some ways you, your family, and your friends can follow through on one idea.

Can you remember a time when you felt hungry? About one billion people in the world are always hungry. This means that one out of five people in the world never get enough food to eat. Many of these people are children. Try to imagine what it is like to just have one cup of boiled rice and water—or even less—as the only food you would eat all day.

Can you write or draw how you would feel?

Having enough clean water for drinking, cooking, and bathing is a global problem. In many places, women and girls must carry most or all of the water needed in their homes over long distances. See if you can carry a container with a small amount of water in it on your head or shoulders for a short distance. Practice until you can walk with this container without dropping it. Then try carrying a pail nearly full of water around a block, a playing field, or a one-acre lot. Could you walk ten times that distance every day? Or, fill two one-gallon milk jugs with water at the start of the day. See if you can last an entire day using only this water for cooking, food preparation, washing, bathing, and flushing the toilet. How did you save water throughout the day? What steps could you continue?

The activities on pages 29–30 are from *Girl Scout Badges and Signs* and *Caring and Coping: Facing Family Crises* Contemporary Issues booklet.

For other global activities, follow the Program Trail.

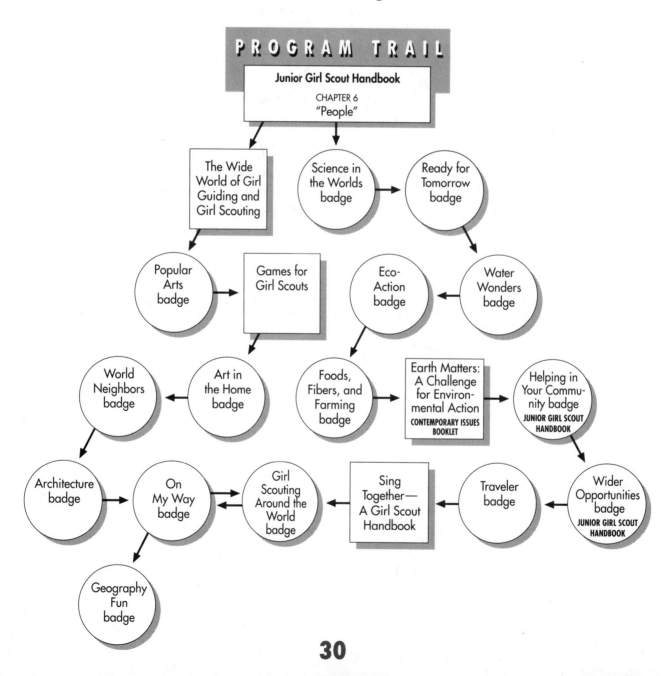

# CHAPTER 4

# HEALTHY EATING AND FITNESS

The way you take care of yourself now will affect you for the rest of your life. Good eating and fitness habits, established early in life and continued into adulthood, have a powerful influence on your health, your appearance, and your emotions. We have all heard that the American diet is too high in fat, sugar, and salt and too low in dietary fiber. Fiber is found in fruits, vegetables, beans, peas, nuts, and in cereal grains such as wheat and rice. Most Americans eat too many processed foods and animal products, which usually contain lots of salt and sugar and fat.

## *Five Steps to Healthful Eating*

**1** Eat plenty of fresh vegetables and fresh fruits. Eat natural foods as much as possible. Use whole or unprocessed grains whenever possible. Select whole wheat breads and pasta instead of white, and use brown rice instead of white rice.

**2** Avoid highly processed convenience foods made with artificial additives and flavorings.

**3** Reduce salt. Use herbs and spices when cooking instead of salt.

**4** Reduce fats. Trim meat of excess fat; remove the skin from poultry. Avoid fried foods, foods cooked with lots of fat or cream, and foods made with whole milk.

**5** Reduce sugar. Avoid drinks and snacks that have a lot of sugar added.

Keep a record of the food you eat for three days. Include any snacks you have. Do your food habits need improving?

|  | DAY ONE | DAY TWO | DAY THREE |
|---|---|---|---|
| Breakfast |  |  |  |
| Lunch |  |  |  |
| Dinner |  |  |  |
| Snack |  |  |  |

Some nutritionists recommend that you eat a balanced diet which includes food from the four food groups. Can you unscramble the foods included in these groups and draw a line connecting the group with its picture? (See bottom of page for answers.)

**1** kilm _____ and
riday _____ products.

**2** dreab _____ ,
leecar _____ , and
saring _____ .

**3** bleatgeves _____ , and
struif _____ .

**4** gleemus _____ ,
team _____ ,
trouply _____ , and
shif _____ .

The activities on pages 31–32 are from *Girl Scout Leader* magazine (Summer 1990), *Girl Scout Badges and Signs*, and the *Junior Girl Scout Handbook*.

For other activities on healthy eating, follow the Program Trail.

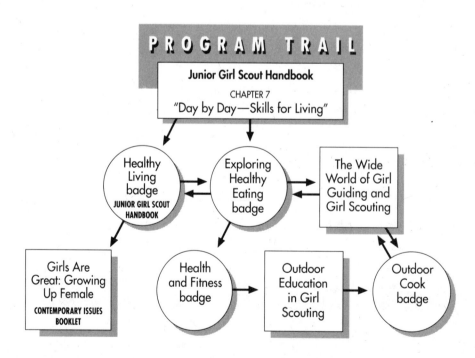

# PROGRAM TRAIL

**Junior Girl Scout Handbook**
CHAPTER 7
"Day by Day—Skills for Living"

Healthy Living badge
JUNIOR GIRL SCOUT HANDBOOK

Exploring Healthy Eating badge

The Wide World of Girl Guiding and Girl Scouting

Girls Are Great: Growing Up Female
CONTEMPORARY ISSUES BOOKLET

Health and Fitness badge

Outdoor Education in Girl Scouting

Outdoor Cook badge

**ANSWER KEY:** 1—Milk and dairy products; 2—Bread, cereal, and grains.
3—Vegetables and fruits; 4—Legumes, meat, poultry, and fish.

When you are eating properly, you can be sure that you are getting the nutrients that your body needs. The basic nutrients in food are:

**Proteins**—the basic building blocks for your body.
**Carbohydrates**—starches and sugar that your body can digest quickly and turn into energy.
**Fats**—nutrients that your body stores for energy later.
**Vitamins and minerals**—nutrients that help make your body work and that prevent certain diseases.
**Water**—a very important part of your body. In fact, your body is more than three-fourths water. Water is in most foods and keeps your body from dehydrating (becoming too dry).

## Testing Foods

The following activities will let you see whether a certain nutrient is present in a food. Only small amounts of food, such as scraps left over from a meal, are needed for these tests.

## Calcium Test

Calcium is a mineral that adds strength and hardness to bones. To test for calcium, you will need a jar, vinegar, and a chicken bone or bits of eggshell. Vinegar removes calcium from bones and shells and softens them. Place the chicken bone or eggshells in a jar and fill it with vinegar. Change the vinegar every two or three days. After two or three weeks, check the hardness of the bones or shell.

## Fat or Oil Test

Foods that have fat or oil (liquid fat) leave a greasy spot on paper because oil and fat seep into the pores and fibers, rather than evaporating as water does. To test for fat or oil, you will need scraps of food and a piece of brown paper. (Buttering or frying foods will add fat to foods, so your test would not be accurate.) Crush a small bit of food on the brown paper. Let the paper dry. If a greasy spot remains, the food contains oil or fat.

What would be your favorite meal? Include everything you might eat at the dinner. With the help of a book on nutrition or other source, find out about your meal. What about salt, fat, and sugar? What are the total of calories this meal would have? Are the nutrients balanced?

## Starch Test

When placed on a food that contains starch, iodine reacts chemically with the starch to form a bluish-black compound. You will need tincture of iodine and scraps of food. Put one drop of tincture of iodine on the food and watch what happens. (Handle iodine carefully. It will stain if it spills and is poisonous if swallowed.)

## Vitamin C Test

Vitamin C reacts chemically with starch and iodine. To test for Vitamin C, you will need cornstarch, water, tincture of iodine, juices, and other liquids. Add one teaspoon of cornstarch to one cup of water and stir to dissolve it. Add 10 drops of tincture of iodine to the cornstarch solution. This will give you the bluish-black liquid you need to test for Vitamin C. Put 10 drops of the bluish-black solution in a cup or small glass and add juice or other liquid, one drop at a time. Stop after 20 drops. If Vitamin C is not present, the color will stay the same. If Vitamin C is present, the solution will lose its color. What happens if you boil a solution that tested positive for Vitamin C? Add it to a test solution after boiling.

The activities on pages 33–34 are from the *Junior Girl Scout Handbook*.

For other activities on foods and nutrition, follow the Program Trail.

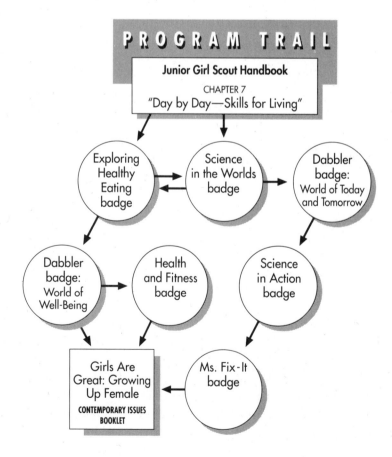

H erbs and spices are used to flavor foods and come in a variety of textures, flavors, colors, and smells. How many names of herbs and spices can you find in this puzzle? Circle the ones you find. Some may be written backwards. (See next page for answers.)

```
S  Y  O  C  H  I  V  E  S  O  E  M  Y  H  T  C  X
A  R  R  H  W  X  L  B  A  L  T  A  S  B  R  A  G
F  A  E  E  S  I  N  A  G  P  A  R  S  L  E  Y  I
F  M  G  R  O  V  U  S  E  C  L  J  V  E  S  E  N
R  E  A  V  L  Z  M  I  N  T  O  O  C  C  K  N  G
O  S  N  I  B  A  Y  L  E  A  F  R  U  R  K  N  E
N  O  O  L  L  I  D  C  A  R  D  A  M  O  N  E  R
P  R  S  L  E  M  O  N  B  A  L  M  I  P  O  Q  R
E  C  I  N  N  A  M  O  N  F  E  N  N  E  L  U  S
D  F  A  T  G  E  M  T  U  N  P  A  P  R  I  K  A
```

Many cultures differ in their use of herbs and spices. Try one or more of these recipes. Create a recipe of your own using at least two or more herbs and spices.

*Peanut Soup from West Africa:*   8 ounces chunky peanut butter, 2 cups chicken broth (or 2 cups of water and 2 bouillon cubes), 1 small onion, chopped, 1 small carrot, chopped in small pieces, 1 stalk of celery chopped in small pieces, red pepper flakes or chili powder to taste, cumin powder to taste. Combine all the ingredients in a saucepan. Stir slowly over low heat until the peanut butter dissolves. Bring to a slow boil, then lower heat and simmer about 20 minutes. Serve over white or brown rice. Cut-up pieces of chicken or beef can be cooked in the soup for an authentic West African dish. Makes 4–6 servings.

*Whole Wheat and Apricot Salad:*   4 ounces bulgur, quinoa, cous-cous, or brown rice, 1 carrot, scrubbed and grated, 2 scallions, chopped, 2 ounces dried apricots, chopped, 1 tablespoon low-fat mayonnaise, 1 tablespoon low-fat plain yogurt, 1 teaspoon freshly chopped parsley, dash of black pepper.

Cook the grains following the directions on the package. Drain and cool. Mix in the apricots, scallions, and carrots; add mayonnaise and yogurt. Sprinkle with parsley and pepper. Serves two.

*String Bean Curry:* 1 pound fresh stringbeans, 1 large onion chopped, 2 tablespoons butter or margarine, ground ginger to taste or grated fresh ginger, 1 teaspoon turmeric, 2 tomatoes, cut in small wedges, 2 potatoes, cut in small pieces, 1 teaspoon lemon juice, curry powder to taste.

String the beans and cut in 1-inch pieces. Heat the butter in a frying pan and fry the onions and ginger until the onions are light golden brown. Add turmeric and fry 2–3 minutes. Add tomatoes. Mix well and cook until most of the liquid has evaporated. Add beans and potatoes. Mix well, cover, and cook over low heat until the beans and potatoes are tender. Add lemon juice and curry powder about 5 minutes before the food is removed from the heat. Makes about 4 servings.

The activities on pages 35–36 are from *The Wide World of Girl Guiding and Girl Scouting* and *Girl Scout Leader* magazine (Summer 1990).

For more activities on healthy recipes, follow the Program Trail.

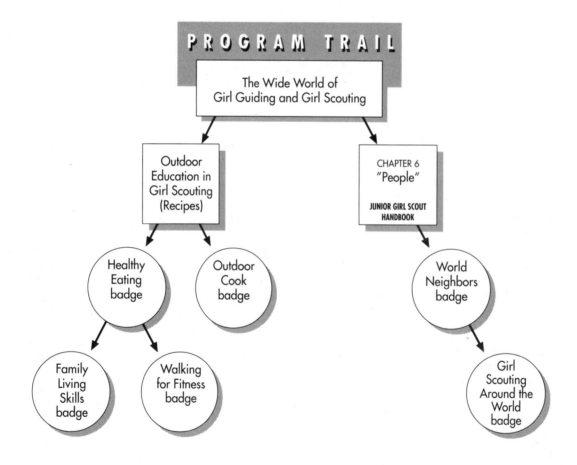

**ANSWER KEY:** anise, basil, bay leaf, chervil, chives, dill, lemon balm, marjoram, mint, oregano, rosemary, sage, parsley, thyme, cardamon, cayenne, cinnamon, cumin, fennel, ginger, nutmeg, paprika, saffron

# BEING PHYSICALLY FIT

**W**hether you are walking, sleeping, playing basketball, or watching television, your body is working and using energy. Good physical fitness can help your body run smoothly and function at its very best. Being fit helps to improve both your health and your appearance.

An important part of fitness is using your muscles to keep them active and strong. You use many muscles every day without thinking. For example:

**Arm muscles**—help you raise your arm to answer a question in class, bend your elbow to throw a ball, move your wrist to brush your teeth
**Leg muscles**—help you run, stand, climb a stair
**Diaphragm muscle**—helps you breathe, talk, sneeze
**Back muscles**—help you stand and sit up and maintain good posture
**Face muscles**—help you smile and frown and express yourself

Exercising regularly is an important way of becoming physically fit. Exercise helps you develop strength, flexibility, and endurance.

## Strength Test

Do some warm-ups first. Push-ups: Lie face down with your hands on the ground outside your shoulders, fingers pointing forward, knees bent. Lift your body by straightening your arms, keeping your back straight. Return to the starting position and repeat. How many push-ups can you do in 30 seconds?

## Flexibility Test

Measure a distance 12 inches (30 centimeters) away from a wall. Mark the spot with a strip of tape. Remove your shoes. Facing the wall, sit on the floor with your legs extended in front of you. Place the heels of your feet on top of the tape. With one hand on top of the other, slowly reach forward. Keep your hands together. How far do you reach? The closer you get to the wall, the more flexible you are.

## Endurance Test

Do some warm-up exercises first. Jumping rope: Jump rope until you get tired. How long can you jump? Walking: Pick a measured area like a school track or jogging trail. See how fast and how far you can walk in 15 minutes. Measure how far you were able to go.

Do you need to get fit? Why not make up your own fitness routine to music? Include friends and family to keep you motivated. Remember to check with a doctor if you do not normally exercise. Activities like dancing, jogging, jumping rope all are good because they help your heart work hard. Include warming-up and cooling-down exercises.

## *My Exercise Plan*

_____

_____

_____

_____

_____

_____

_____

_____

The activities on pages 37–38 are from the *Junior Girl Scout Handbook* and *Girl Scout Leader* magazine (Winter 1990).

For more activities on fitness, follow the Program Trail.

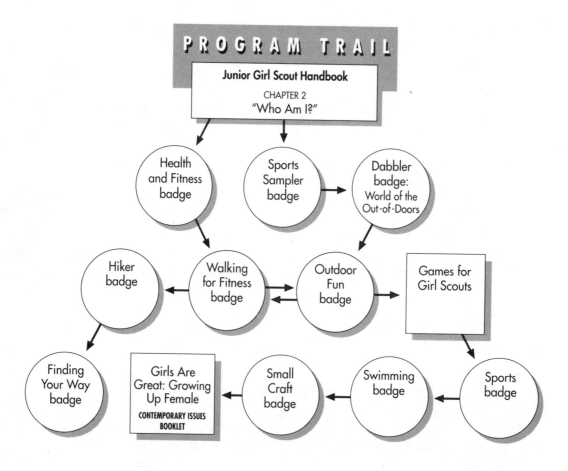

**PROGRAM TRAIL**

**Junior Girl Scout Handbook**
CHAPTER 2
"Who Am I?"

- Health and Fitness badge
- Sports Sampler badge
- Dabbler badge: World of the Out-of-Doors
- Hiker badge
- Walking for Fitness badge
- Outdoor Fun badge
- Games for Girl Scouts
- Finding Your Way badge
- Girls Are Great: Growing Up Female **CONTEMPORARY ISSUES BOOKLET**
- Small Craft badge
- Swimming badge
- Sports badge

ake a list of games that you enjoy that include aerobic activity. Basketball, roller or ice skating, jumping rope, field hockey, tennis, tag, soccer, or softball are all examples.

## Pyramid Soccer

You will need three to five plastic bottles and one soccer or kick ball.

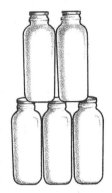

How to play: Arrange the bottles to form a pyramid in the middle of a circle. One girl is designated "goalie" and must defend the pyramid. Form a circle and kick the ball toward the center and try to knock the pyramid down. The girl who knocks the pyramid down becomes the new "goalie."

## Stocking Badminton

You will need a wire coat hanger, one leg of a pair of pantyhose, masking tape, and scissors.

Bend the hanger into a diamond shape. Bend the hook of the hanger to form a handle. Slowly pull the foot of the hose over the hanger down to the handle. Wrap the leg of the hose around the handle. Tape the hose to the handle. Cut off any extra hose. You can use a badminton "birdie" or a ball made of foam or sponge. Try this game with a friend or a group. See how long you can keep the "birdie" in the air!

## Scooper Ball

You will need a one-gallon plastic bottle with a handle.

Cut the bottle according to this diagram. Decorate your bottle with felt pens. Using a small ball, try:

- Throwing the ball in the air and catching it with the scooper.
- Standing in a circle and tossing the ball back and forth using the scooper.
- Setting up a "scooper ball" court with boundaries. Play scooper-volleyball!

## Sardines

How to play: Divide into pairs. One pair are "hiders." Hiders have two minutes in which to hide. The other pairs then set out to find them. Partners must stay together. When partners find hiders, they join them in their hiding place. This continues until all the partners have found the hiders. The first partners to find the hiders become the hiders for the next game.

## Follow the Leader

How to play this jump rope game: Jumpers stand in line in front of the rope. Two players turn the rope. The leader jumps in with the turn and repeats a rhyme of her choice before jumping out. The next girl must jump in and repeat the rhyme while jumping and then exit. If she can't repeat the rhyme exactly, she must take the place of one of the turners.

## Rock the Cradle

How to play this jump rope game: The rope turners allow the rope to swing back and forth in a low arc, just brushing the ground. Each girl in turn must jump the rope two or three times and jump out without catching the rope in her feet. When everyone has had a turn, the rope is raised a few more inches and the round is repeated. Raise the rope a little higher each time. The girl who can complete all the rounds successfully is the winner.

The activities on pages 39–40 are from *Games for Girl Scouts* and the *Junior Girl Scout Handbook*.

For other activities on sports and games, follow the program trail.

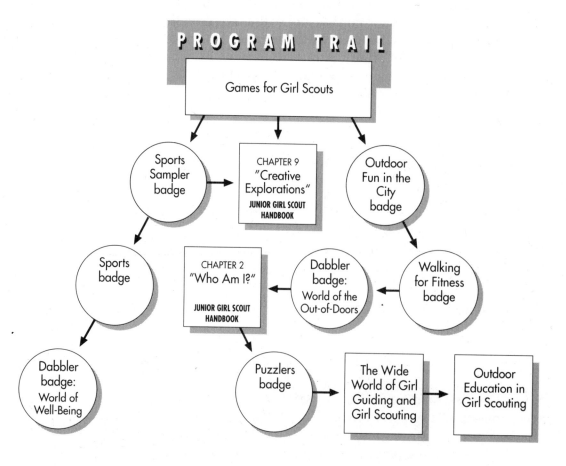

ave you ever noticed the following?

- A rainbow forms in the sky after a spring rain.
- A bicycle left outside will start to rust.
- An opened bottle of soda pop left overnight loses its fizz.

The spark of science, math, and technology is a search for the what, why, and how of things. Science does not take place just in a laboratory or through calculating long formulas. Science and math are everywhere and everyone can be a scientist in action!

## Science Scavenger Hunt

| LOOK FOR: | WHAT, WHY, HOW |
|---|---|
| A greenish-blue metal statue, light post, building sign | Copper reacts with oxygen in the air and a greenish-blue tarnish forms on the metal. |

A bird's feather

Feathers protect birds. See how the parts of a feather are connected.

A rock with layers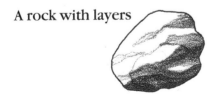

Some rocks were formed when layers of mud, silt, and sand hardened millions of years ago.

A rainbow pattern of light

Sunlight is actually made up of many colors that look white to our eyes. When white light passes through certain clear things like a prism, raindrops, or a bubble, it is broken into its many colors.

Steam

Heat can turn liquid water into a gas (steam).

Make up your own list of things to find with friends.

Try these activities. Watch what happens.

*Eye Changes:*   Try this with a friend. Cup your hand over one open eye for a minute. Quickly pull your hand away. Watch how the pupil, the dark center of the eye, reacts to light.

*Plants Drinking Water:*   Cut the bottom end off a stalk of celery. Put it in a glass of water colored blue or red with food coloring. Watch what happens.

*Surface Tension:*   Using a fork, carefully lay a paper clip flat on the surface of water in a bowl. Add several drops of dishwashing detergent.

*Water Drop Magnifier:*   Cut a piece of clear plastic wrap that is about four inches square. Place this on a book or newspaper. Using an eye dropper, put a small drop of water on the plastic wrap. Look at the paper through the drop of water.

The activities on pages 41–42 are from the *Junior Girl Scout Handbook.*

For other activities on science experiments, follow the Program Trail.

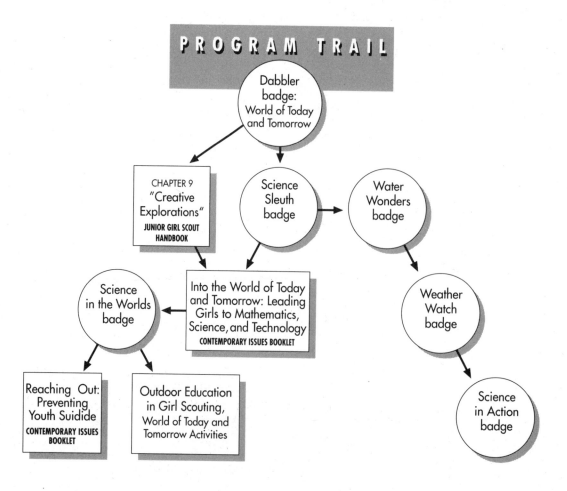

PROGRAM TRAIL

Dabbler badge: World of Today and Tomorrow

CHAPTER 9 "Creative Explorations" **JUNIOR GIRL SCOUT HANDBOOK**

Science Sleuth badge

Water Wonders badge

Science in the Worlds badge

Into the World of Today and Tomorrow: Leading Girls to Mathematics, Science, and Technology **CONTEMPORARY ISSUES BOOKLET**

Weather Watch badge

Reaching Out: Preventing Youth Suicide **CONTEMPORARY ISSUES BOOKLET**

Outdoor Education in Girl Scouting, World of Today and Tomorrow Activities

Science in Action badge

T hink of all the things you use every day that rely on technology to work. Make a list of at least ten things that could be hard to live without. Ask your friends to make lists. Do you depend on the same technologies? Some people might be able to live without automatic bank cards but absolutely depend upon a cordless phone. Other might not need a dishwasher, but could not live without a television. What are your ten necessities?

1 _____

2 _____

3 _____

4 _____

5 _____

6 _____

7 _____

8 _____

9 _____

10 _____

Which of these existed ten years ago? fifty years ago? one hundred years ago?

How do you think these technologies will have changed one hundred years from now?

Learn how to do one of the following with an adult as a partner and demonstrate your knowledge to a friend or family member:

- Hook up a VCR machine and program it to record a TV program the next day.
- Format a disc, create a file, print stored information, and save something you have created on a personal computer.
- Run a safety check on a car. Include the tires, battery, lights, turn signals, emergency flashers, back-up lights, windshield wipers, fluids and oil, spare tire, jack, and flares.
- Make a simple repair on a small appliance in your home.
- Make and test-fly three different types of paper airplanes. Be able to explain their differences in flight.

The activities on pages 43–44 are from *Into the World of Today and Tomorrow: Leading Girls to Mathematics, Science, and Technology* Contemporary Issues booklet, *Girl Scout Badges and Signs*, and the *Junior Girl Scout Handbook*.

For other activities on technology, follow the Program Trail.

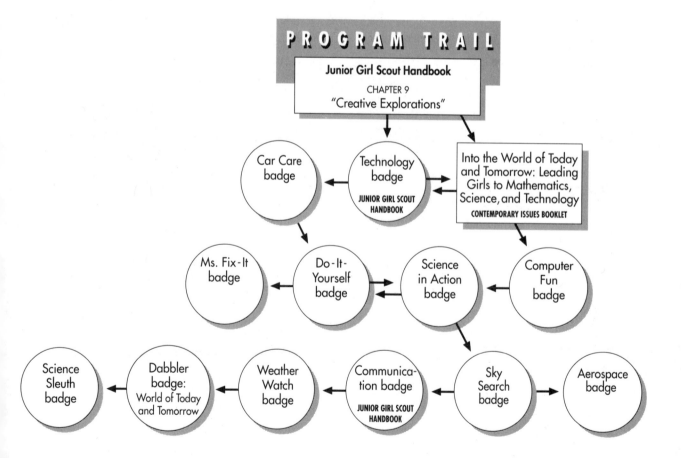

## PUZZLERS

**C**an you solve these riddles?

**1** How can you throw a ball so that it always comes back?

**2** Which weighs more, a pound of rocks or a pound of feathers?

**3** Which side of the roof will the rooster's egg roll down?

**4** What is worse than finding a worm in an apple?

**5** When is a penny more than a dime?

**6** Which horizontal line is longer?

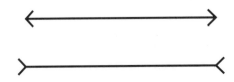

Try writing your name on a piece of paper while you are tracing circles on the floor with your foot.

Stare at this picture. Do you see a young woman or an old woman?

The activities on pages 45–46 are from the *Junior Girl Scout Handbook* and *Girl Scout Badges and Signs*.

For more activities on puzzlers, follow the Program Trail.

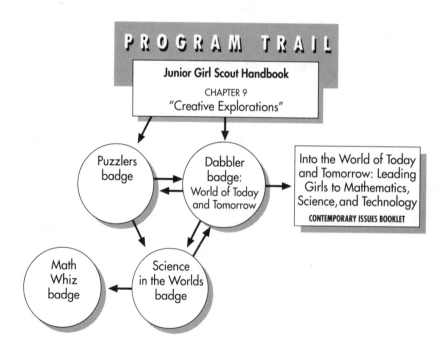

**ANSWER KEY:** 1—Straight up. Gravity will bring the ball back to you. 2—They both weigh one pound. 3—Neither; roosters don't lay eggs. 4—Finding half a worm in an apple. 5—When you weigh them. 6—The lines are exactly the same size.

# HUMAN CALCULATORS

There are not too many things that a penny can buy, but you can use a penny to test the theory of probability. Flip a penny. Can you predict how many times "heads" will show and how many times "tails" will show? The theory of probability states that heads will probably show one out of every two times you flip the penny. Try flipping a penny repeatedly. What happens?

## Bees and Wasps

Bees and wasps both want to take over this hive. Who is going to win?

Bees are B and wasps are W. The bee and the wasp take turns marking a B or a W in one honeycomb of the hive. The winner is the first bee or wasp to complete a path connecting her two sides of the hive. The corner honeycombs belong to both the bees and the wasps.

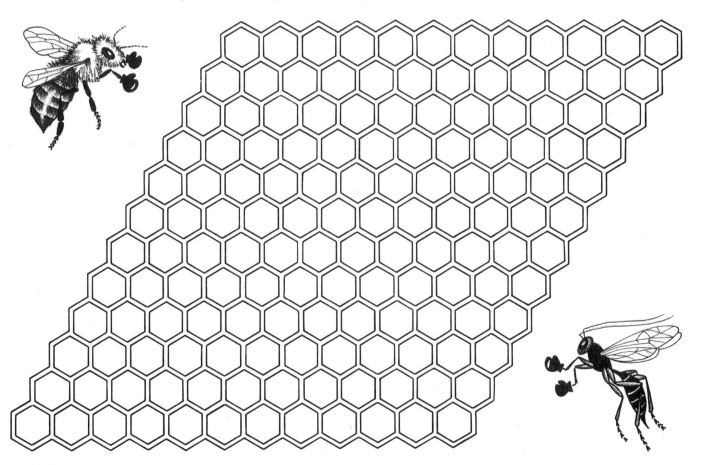

Are there ways to improve your chances of winning? Would ways to win change if the winner were the one with the most honeycombs? Try your own versions of the game.

Have a contest to find out who can calculate most accurately the number of objects of a similar size that can fit into a large container. Choose the container and the objects, such as popcorn, beans, or marbles. Let the contestants measure the container and a small number of objects and then calculate their answers. Give an award to the winner(s).

Play a game that involves logic and strategic thinking (a method of careful planning). The game could be chess or checkers, or another board game. Play the game at least five times. Each time you play, make notes about what helps to win the game. Are there moves to avoid, or a sequence of steps to take? Play the game again after you have reviewed your notes and see if your skill improves.

The activities on pages 47–48 are from the *Junior Girl Scout Handbook*, Chapter 9, "Creative Explorations," and *Girl Scout Badges and Signs*.

For other mathematical activities, follow the Program Trail.

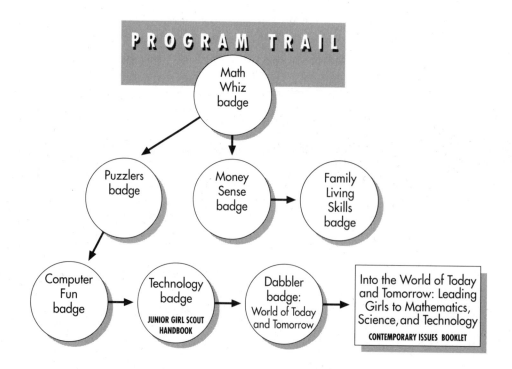

PROGRAM TRAIL

Math Whiz badge

Puzzlers badge

Money Sense badge

Family Living Skills badge

Computer Fun badge

Technology badge
JUNIOR GIRL SCOUT HANDBOOK

Dabbler badge: World of Today and Tomorrow

Into the World of Today and Tomorrow: Leading Girls to Mathematics, Science, and Technology
CONTEMPORARY ISSUES BOOKLET

Wherever you live, going outdoors can provide many adventures. Some outdoor experiences are simple, like discovering unusual plants in a parking lot. Some involve much planning and preparation, like going on a camping trip. Whatever you do in the outdoors, you should plan ahead, dress right, keep safe, and walk softly.

## Planning Ahead

Everything you do is usually more successful if you plan ahead. The planning you need to do depends upon what you will do and how much experience you have had. Some trips might need special clothing, equipment, or food. You might need to know how to tell directions or how to follow a trail.

## Dressing Right

Wearing the right clothes for an outdoor activity is very important. Some activities can even be dangerous if you wear the wrong clothes. You need to dress to stay warm or to stay cool and to protect yourself from the sun.

## Keeping Safe

Everyone should learn basic safety rules. Some important outdoor ones are to know about the poisonous plants and animals in your area, to know the symptoms and treatments for hypothermia (low body temperature) and heat exhaustion (high body temperature), to be prepared for weather emergencies, to never leave the group, to know what to do if you should become lost.

## Walking Softly

Millions of living things call the outdoors home. Plants and animals live in a special balance. Be careful not to disturb the environment. Always try to leave a place in the same condition or better than you found it.

Get to know more about the wildlife in your community. Choose one animal, large or small, and find out about its life history. Paste or draw a picture of it on a sheet of paper. What role does it play in your community? How does it affect your life? (Think hard. Every animal or plant on earth somehow affects your life.)

Imagine you are one of the girls in the picture on page 50. What do you see? How do you feel? What do you hear?

The activities on pages 49–50 are from the *Junior Girl Scout Handbook,* *Outdoor Education in Girl Scouting*, and *Earth Matters: A Challenge for Environmental Action* Contemporary Issues booklet.

For more activities on preparation for outdoor adventures, follow the Program Trail.

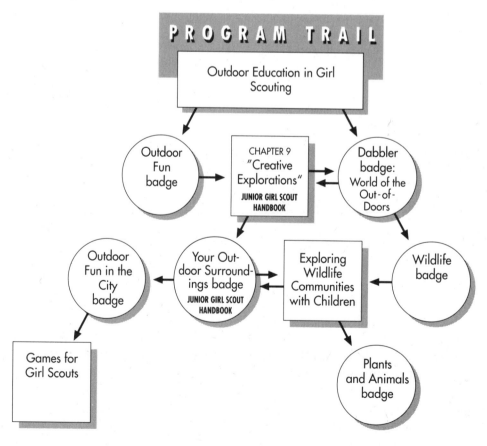

It is important to know where you are going and how to get home when you are exploring nature. The sun or stars can be used to find directions. In the morning, the sun is in the east. If you stand with your left shoulder toward the sun, you will be facing south. In the afternoon, the sun is in the west. If you stand with your left shoulder toward the sun, you will be facing north. Whenever you are facing north, the east is to your right, the west is to your left, and south is behind you. At night, Polaris, the North Star, can be used to help you find north. The easiest way to find Polaris is to locate the Big Dipper.

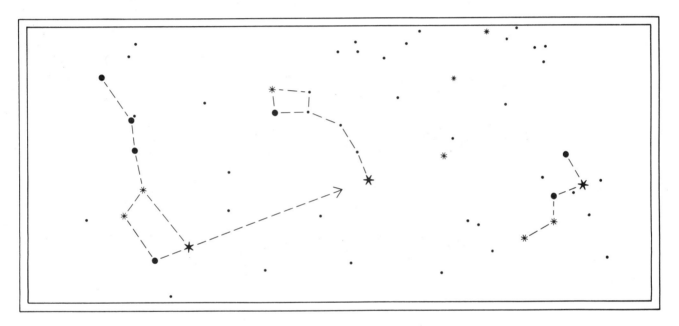

Mapping directions is another way to show people how to get from one place to another. A sketch map is the type you can make easily. You will need a "legend"—a list of what the symbols on your map mean. Here are some examples of symbols.

Railroad            School

Trees            River

A sketch map should be drawn to scale to give an idea of distance. For example, you might make 1 inch = 35 paces. Knowing your pace is a good way to measure distances. A pace is two steps. Mark off a distance of 330 feet (100 meters). Walk it five times, counting the paces. Try to walk naturally. How many paces do you average? Divide 100 meters by the number of paces. This gives you the length of one pace. Now you can measure any distance on the ground.

Choose a part of your community that you know well. Draw a sketch map of it here. Include a legend and scale. See if others can recognize your map.

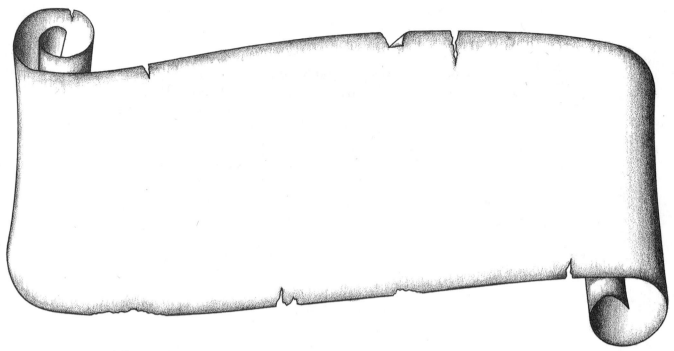

The activities on pages 51–52 are from the *Junior Girl Scout Handbook* and *Outdoor Education in Girl Scouting*.

For other activities on finding your way, follow the Program Trail.

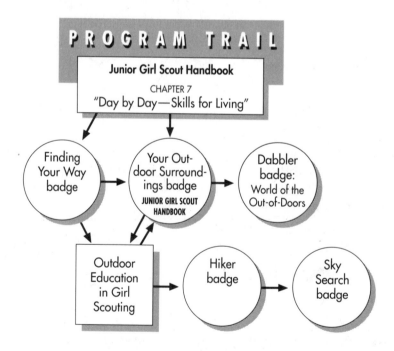

# EXPLORING NATURE WITH OUR SENSES

Our senses help us to be detectives in our environment. Our senses help us tune our brains, see more clearly, and remember more. We become more aware of what is around us. We can appreciate what is around us all the more.

## Seeing

Take a wire coat hanger and stretch it into a circle. Put it on the ground. Examine carefully what you find inside. Make a list of what you see.

Lie on your stomach and look down. Lie on your back and look up.

Look for shapes. How many squares, circles, and triangles can you find?

Find a design or scene that you especially like. Draw it, sketch it, or take a photograph.

## Listening

Sit down and blindfold your eyes. Can you hear these sounds:

Day sounds, night sounds, sounds of the season, sounds you like and sounds you dislike, sad sounds, happy sounds, peaceful or noisy sounds.

Record your sounds on a tape recorder, on a song that you create, or on a piece of music that reminds you of these sounds.

## Feeling

How many different textures can you discover in one small area?

Feel something with your fingers, the back of your hands, and your cheek.

Feel something in a paper bag. Can you describe it without seeing it?

Can you feel the wind? How would you describe it?

How can you feel the sun? shade?

## Smelling

Breathe deeply. What can you smell?

Can you tell the difference between artificial smells and natural smells?

Follow a scent; where does it lead?

What does rain smell like? How does the outdoors smell after it rains? snows?

Pinch a leaf, a root, some dirt. What smells come out?

What smells do you like? Which ones don't you like?

## My Observations

| DATE | SEEING | LISTENING | FEELING | SMELLING |
|------|--------|-----------|---------|----------|
|      |        |           |         |          |
|      |        |           |         |          |
|      |        |           |         |          |
|      |        |           |         |          |
|      |        |           |         |          |
|      |        |           |         |          |

The activities on pages 53–54 are from *Exploring Wildlife Communities with Children* and *Girl Scout Badges and Signs*.

For other activities on exploring the outdoors, follow the Program Trail.

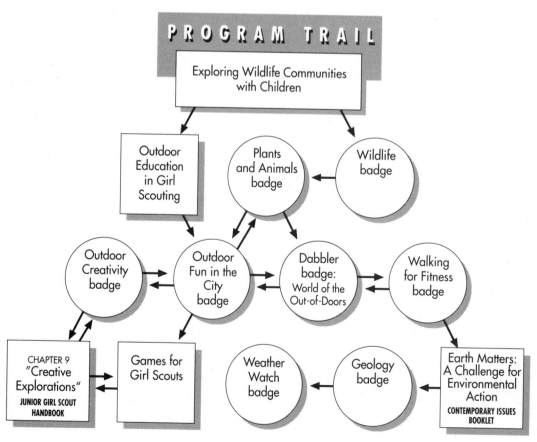

## ENVIRONMENTAL ACTION

If you looked at the Planet Earth from outer space, you would see a very fragile atmosphere that surrounds the Earth on which people and man-made things are a very small part. All parts of life on the Earth—plants and animals—depend upon each other in order to exist. Plants are essential to maintaining life—they are a part of the water cycle and they take in carbon dioxide and add oxygen, which animals need, to the air. Animals use plants as food sources. Animals also use water, absorb and give off heat, and contribute carbon dioxide and other waste products to the environment. Plant and animal decomposers break down and recycle organic waste and make the parts available for new life to grow. All life depends upon the sun. Plants need sunlight to make food. The sun's energy affects weather and climate. All the living things that interact are called an ecosystem. Air, water, soil, energy, open space and natural areas, garbage and solid waste, and the quality of life—how we live—are all parts of the Earth's ecosystem that need to be protected to keep life healthy on this planet.

A credo is a group of beliefs or principles that you promise to live by. How do you interact with the environment? How can you protect it? Write your personal credo here.

I believe _____

_____

_____

How can you incorporate your credo into your daily actions?

Think of three things you can do to protect the environment.

**1** _____

**2** _____

**3** _____

Find a safe corner in your community where you can make a traffic survey. Count the number of vehicles that pass by in 30 minutes at three different times a day. Keep track of how many different vehicles only carry one person. How could you encourage more efficient use of transportation?

Find out how to read your electric meter. Compile a list of items in your home that use electricity. Which appliances use electricity at the fastest rate? Find out ways to consume less energy in your home.

Find out what your community does to preserve the environment. Does your community have a recycling program? ways to prevent soil erosion? water conservation or clean water laws? air pollution regulations? List what you have discovered here.

The activities on pages 55–56 are from *Earth Matters: A Challenge for Environmental Action* Contemporary Issues booklet and *Girl Scout Badges and Signs*.

For other activities on the environment, follow the Program Trail.

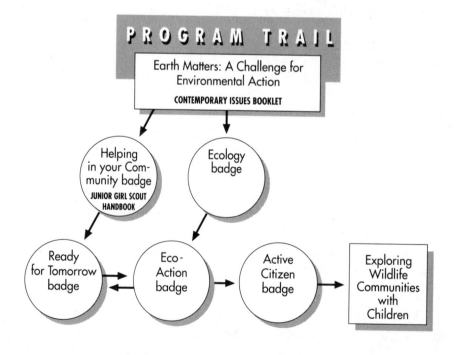

 **E**veryone can be creative. You don't have to be a great artist or composer. Just use your imagination to explore the world around you.

 Everyone can create art. The creation can be a drawing, a piece of music, a dance, or a poem—anything that adds beauty or pleasure to the world. Art can be used to express feelings about life or to send messages to people.

What messages do you pick up in the music you listen to or in the books you read? What about the sculptures or buildings that you see? Different people react differently to a particular piece of art. You might love a song while someone else may hate it. A painting that is beautiful to you may be nothing special to someone else. Art can help you see how others look at the world, and art can help you understand yourself and your feelings.

Art can be part of ceremonies and religions. Art can be part of holidays and celebrations. Art can be a window to discover what is beautiful and valuable in other cultures. In this window, draw, paint, or make a collage that would show others by looking in the window what is beautiful and valuable to you.

Find out about primary and secondary colors. Make a color wheel and explain it to others. What are complementary colors? Practice mixing colors to make new ones. Create a picture using all of the colors on a color wheel. Create a picture or design using just complementary colors.

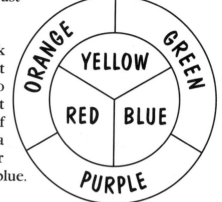

You can make many shades of the same color. Look at something that is mostly one color. Notice that light and shadow can change the basic color into different shades. Make a picture of something that is mostly one color. Some examples are hills full of trees that are many shades of green, buildings in a city that are many shades of brick red or gray, or curtains on a window that are different shades of blue.

Look through magazines and catalogs. Get permission to cut out shapes in different shades of the same color. Make a one-color collage.

The activities on pages 57–58 are from the *Junior Girl Scout Handbook* and *Girl Scout Badges and Signs*.

For other activities on art and color, follow the Program Trail.

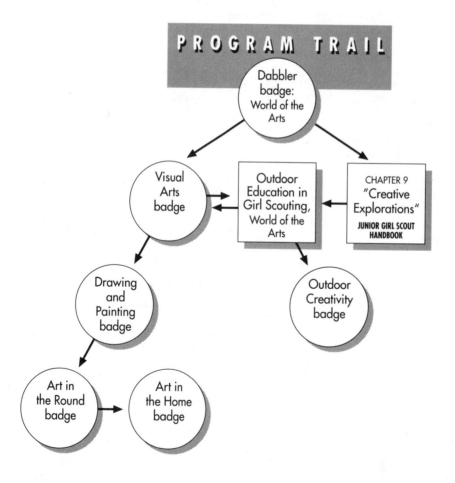

isten to several songs. Do some of the following activities:

- Choose one that you feel is good for dancing. Create a dance for you and a group to do in time to the music.
- Create a design or picture that expresses what the music is saying.
- Create a poem or story inspired by the music.

Create one or both of the following instruments. Use them to beat out the rhythm of the songs.

Castanets are often used by Spanish dancers when they dance the flamenco. You can make your own with two rectangular pieces of wood or blocks shaped like this. The two pieces must be narrow enough that you can hold both in one hand. Wrap a thick rubber band around the ends of the two pieces of wood and put a toothpick or other small, round stick between the two pieces of wood approximately ⅓–½ inch from the rubber band. Now click the two pieces of wood together in rhythm.

Make a West African rhythm instrument usually used by women at ceremonies and festivals. Find a stick that looks like this or make a Y shape out of wood or a small hanger. Collect bottle caps, round flat metal washers, or other light metal round objects or round flat shells or beads that have holes or can be drilled to make holes in their middles. String your objects on cord, heavy-duty coat thread, or plastic line. Leave about two or three inches of cord bare and tie the ends tightly around the top of the Y, like this. You have a rattle that you can shake as an accompanying instrument, or you can make up your own music.

Learn the words and music to this song. Try singing it in a round. A round is when different people or groups of people sing the same song in a circle, each starting at a different time. What other rounds can you sing?

# WHENE'ER YOU MAKE A PROMISE
## (Four-part Round)

W. W. SHIELD, 1828

When e'er you make a prom-ise Con-sid-er well its im-port-ance And when made, en-grave it up-on your heart.

The activities on pages 59–60 are from *Girl Scout Badges and Signs* and the *Girl Scout Pocket Songbook*.

For other activities on music, follow the Program Trail.

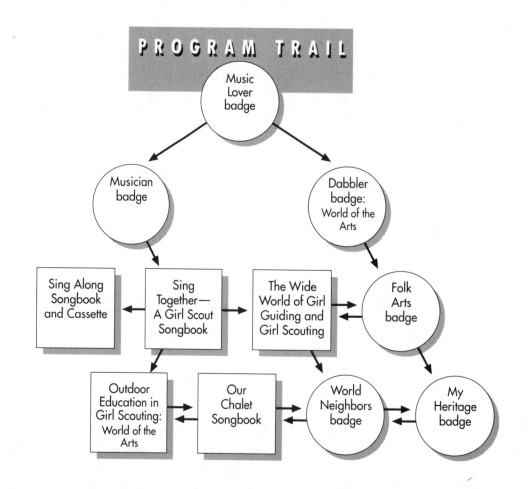

## EXPRESSING YOURSELF THROUGH DRAMA AND DANCE

**T**ry these creative techniques:

Actresses make the audience believe that the characters they portray are real. Try being an actress. Look in a mirror and practice facial expressions that show emotions. Can you show joy, happiness sadness, fear, surprise, boredom, excitement, and anger?

Try to "mirror mimic" with someone else. While facing each other, one person must copy everything the other person (the leader) does. Take turns being the leader. Try to be mirror images.

Say "I did it" five times, expressing a different emotion each time: for example, pride, guilt, fear, happiness, surprise, or horror. See if other people can guess which emotion you are expressing.

Be a mime. A mime acts without speaking. Create a pantomime based on a reaction to something: taste something delicious/bitter, touch something hot/cold, see something beautiful/horrible, smell something sweet/rotten.

Do an improvisation (a skit with no practice) with a small group based on suggestions from the audience.

Pretend to have a conversation on the phone with an imaginary person. See if your audience can guess what the other "person" is saying.

Use pantomime to show at least five different ways a person can feel: lazy, sad, energetic, happy, sick, frightened, in love, or bored.

Demonstrate in body movements the following:

- The feelings that a particular piece of music brings out in you.
- The ways different people move (athletes, waiters, young people, old people, traffic conductors, cooks, musicians, etc.).
- An expression of nature, such as trees moving in the wind, rocks rolling down a hill, or volcanoes erupting.

Try creating a dance to music based on one of the above types of movements.

With friends, create a short play or skit from a familiar story. Make a list of the important events in the story. Decide which events you'll show in a scene and how many scenes you'll have. List the characters. Decide who will play each part. Make up dialogue, movements, voices, and gestures that suit the characters. Use a narrator to present your scenes. Try creating simple costumes.

The activities on pages 61–62 are from *Girl Scout Badges and Signs*.

For other activities on drama and dance, follow the Program Trail.

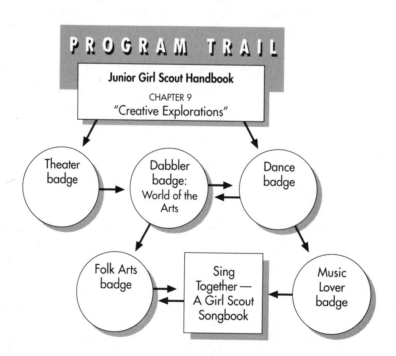

PROGRAM TRAIL

Junior Girl Scout Handbook
CHAPTER 9
"Creative Explorations"

Theater badge

Dabbler badge: World of the Arts

Dance badge

Folk Arts badge

Sing Together — A Girl Scout Songbook

Music Lover badge

You can use words to describe how you feel or what you see. You can keep your writing secret or you can share your creations with others. Sit in a quiet place, indoors or outdoors. Choose an object that appeals to you. Examine it. What makes this object different from all others? Look at it closely. Use your senses. Now close your eyes and imagine how it would feel to *be* this object. What would your skin be like? your voice? What would you think about? How would you see the world? What things would be important to you? Try writing a poem or short story from this object's point of view.

_____

_____

_____

_____

_____

International Children's Book Day

April 2nd is International Children's Book Day. This day was chosen because a very famous author of children's fairy tales and stories was born on this day in 1805. Two of his most famous stories are "The Ugly Duckling" and "The Emperor's New Clothes." Can you unscramble his name? (See next page for answer.)

### SHAN SCHARTINI DREANNES

_ _ _ _   _ _ _ _ _ _ _ _   _ _ _ _ _ _ _ _

Think of a way you could celebrate International Children's Book Day.

Pretend you are a traveler from outer space visiting earth for the first time. Your assignment is to find a special spot and describe it so it can be reproduced on your planet. Record your impressions in a notebook. You only have 30 minutes. Your mission is not to startle the inhabitants or interfere with the ecosystem. Report on the shapes, colors, sounds, smells, and interactions of things.

Become a publishing tycoon! Start a newsletter or short magazine. Include pictures, drawings, and cartoons along with written items. Look at magazines and newspapers for ideas for articles and ways of arranging your printed text (the written part). Try to "publish" at least four editions.

The activities on pages 63–64 are from the *Junior Girl Scout Handbook* and *Girl Scout Badges and Signs*.

For more activities on expressing yourself through words, follow the Program Trail.

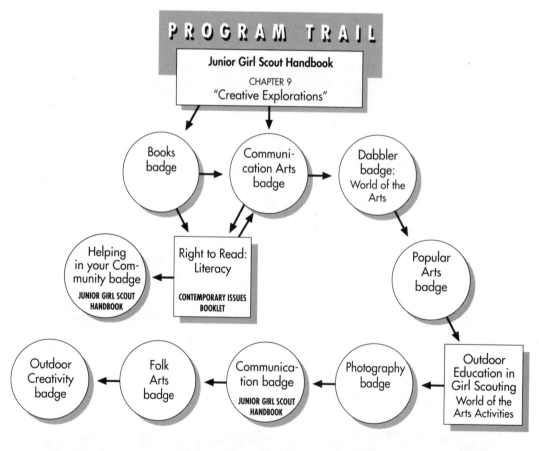

**ANSWER KEY:** Hans Christian Andersen

**W**hich brands of jeans should I buy? Should I tell my friend Rona that I'm angry with her? What can I do about my shyness? Should I invite Juana or Michelle over for the weekend? How do I let Rafael know that I like him? How can I tell my Mom that my older sister started smoking?

These kinds of questions don't have a single answer. They are different from the questions your teacher may ask in math class. When she asks you how much is 8 multiplied by 4, you know that the answer is 32. But questions like the ones above require decisions—choices must be made among many possible answers. In fact, there may not always be one right answer.

You make choices every day. And, as you grow older, you will continue to make many choices. You might decide what kind of work you want to do, where you would live, whom you would marry. It is never too soon to start thinking about how you make decisions and to start practicing for bigger decisions now.

Sometimes it seems that only adults make decisions. That is not true. You make decisions every day about many things. When you chose the clothes you would wear this morning or how you would style your hair, you were making decisions.

Some decisions are easy. Some people have an easier time making decisions than others. When Ashley is asked by her friends which movie she wants to see, she decides in a second! When Doreen is asked the same question, she goes through all the reasons she might want to see one film, then all the reasons she might want to see the other. Then she thinks about her first reasons again! By the time she is ready to make a decision, her friends are already at the movies!

Are you more like Ashley or Doreen?

Active decision-making gives you more power, more control over your life, and greater confidence in yourself. Sally doesn't take advantage of her decision-making opportunities.

On Tuesday morning, Sally woke up late. Her mother didn't call to wake her up. Practically all she had time to do was brush her teeth and throw on the first clothes her mother got ready for her. She didn't have time to eat breakfast or pick an outfit she felt good wearing. She rushed off to school hungry and in a bad mood.

Rewrite this story so that she is an active decision-maker.

_____

_____

_____

_____

_____

The activities on pages 65–66 are from the *Junior Girl Scout Handbook*.

For more activities on decision-making, follow the Program Trail.

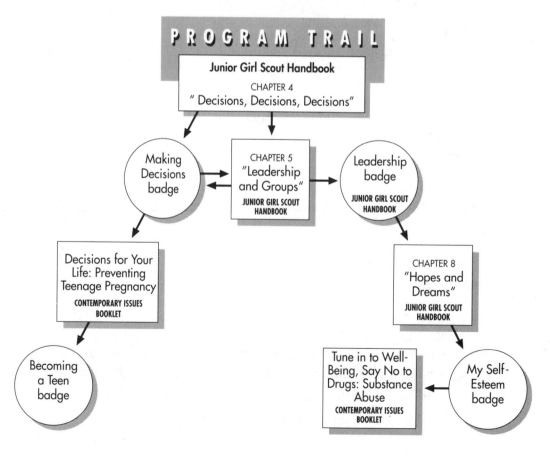

PROGRAM TRAIL

Junior Girl Scout Handbook
CHAPTER 4
"Decisions, Decisions, Decisions"

Making Decisions badge

CHAPTER 5 "Leadership and Groups"
JUNIOR GIRL SCOUT HANDBOOK

Leadership badge
JUNIOR GIRL SCOUT HANDBOOK

Decisions for Your Life: Preventing Teenage Pregnancy
CONTEMPORARY ISSUES BOOKLET

CHAPTER 8 "Hopes and Dreams"
JUNIOR GIRL SCOUT HANDBOOK

Becoming a Teen badge

Tune in to Well-Being, Say No to Drugs: Substance Abuse
CONTEMPORARY ISSUES BOOKLET

My Self-Esteem badge

# STEPS TO A DECISION

Volleyball
Piano
Cheerleading
Dance
Computers
Japanese

How do you make decisions? There are steps you can follow that will help you. You may not use all these steps for every decision, but they are good to remember when you must make a big decision. Here's how Lee went through the steps.

It's the first day of sixth grade. Each student has been asked to choose one after-school activity. There is a long list of choices — piano, volleyball, cheerleading, computer class, modern dance, Japanese lessons. Lee must let her teacher know her choice by the end of the day.

## Step 1: Know the Problem or Issue

Lee needs to pick an activity. If she doesn't choose, her teacher will choose for her. What does Lee want to gain from her after-school experience?

## Step 2: Collect Information About Yourself and the Situation

Lee needs to examine her values, her talents, her interests, and her goals. Is spending extra time in an activity with her friends more important than learning the piano? Does she want to start a new hobby or learn more about something she already knows? Is she interested in exercise or music?

## Step 3: Think of All the Ways the Problem Could Be Solved

Lee should think of as many solutions as possible.

- She could choose piano and schedule other afternoons to spend with her friends.
- She could convince her friends to join the volleyball team and get in good shape together.

It is important to think of as many solutions as possible without criticizing any of them. A solution that seems silly at first could turn out to be the best idea later.

## Step 4: Look at the Good and Bad Points of Each Idea

How well does each idea fit in with your goals and interests and values? Is it practical? Maybe Lee's friends hate volleyball.

**67**

## Step 5: Make a Decision

After looking at all the information, it is time to make a choice. Lee decides on the piano lessons. She can get into good physical shape by exercising at home or with her friends and see her friends at other times. Piano lessons she cannot do on her own.

## Step 6: Take Action

Now that the decision has been made, take action. Lee tells her teacher her choice. She also talks to her friends and sets up an exercise group twice a week. They'll take turns meeting at each other's houses and choosing the exercise music and routines.

## Step 7: See If You Are Happy with the Decision

You may think that once the decision has been made, your work is over. Sometimes, though, you need to look at a decision again. The choice you made may have been right at the time, but later you may need a new decision.

Lee loved taking piano lessons for three months, but her teacher was transferred to a new school and her new teacher was not nearly as patient or good. Lee thought that it might be time for a new decision.

The activities on pages 67–68 are from the *Junior Girl Scout Handbook*.

For more activities on decision-making, follow the Program Trail.

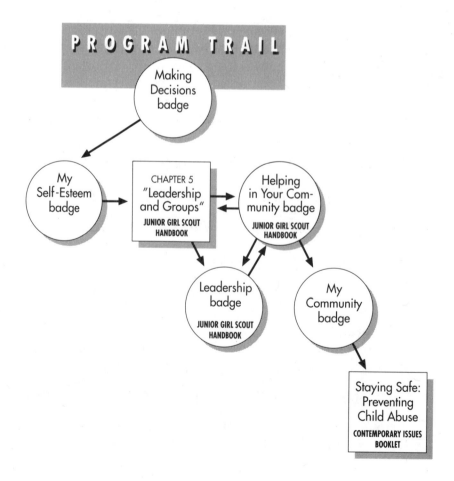

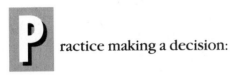
**P**ractice making a decision:

*Step 1:* My problem is _____

_____

*Step 2:* Collect information about myself (values, interests, skills) and the situation.

_____

_____

_____

*Step 3:* Think of all the ways to solve the problem:

_____

_____

_____

_____

_____

_____

*Step 4:* Think about the good and bad points of each possible solution.

*Step 5:* My decision is _____

_____

_____

*Step 6:* Take action — I will do these things next.

_____

_____

_____

*Step 7:* In three months I will look at my decision again. Will things have changed? Do I need to make another decision?

## *Making Decisions About Time*

Because you will never have enough time to do everything you'd like to do, you will always have to make decisions about how to spend your time. Think of all the things you would like to do today. . . . How many do you have the time to actually do? You will have to make some decisions. Try these ways to manage your time.

Make a list of what you need or want to get done. This "To Do" list could be for one afternoon, for one day, or for one week. Writing everything you need to do can help you plan your time. Once you have made your list, put a * next to the most important things. Try to do these first. Are any of the things on the list unnecessary? Cross those off. Could someone else help you or even do these things for you? Cross those items off the list. Start accomplishing things. You'll feel much better once you see how much you have gotten done.

What is your best time for getting things done? Some people are morning people. They get up early with lots of energy and start working right away. Other people are night people. They have a hard time getting up in the morning, but once the afternoon comes, they have lots of energy and can work right into the evening. Plan your most difficult work or things that need lots of concentration for the time of day that you are the most alert.

Try to plan ahead. If you know that you must finish something by a certain time, do not leave the project until the last minute. That is called procrastination. Procrastination is a very difficult habit to break. Once you have left everything to be done until the last possible moment, you will feel stressed out, you won't have time to handle problems you didn't think would occur, and you can't do as good a job as you could have. Try breaking the job into smaller pieces and schedule a piece of the job to do every day. Write it on your "To Do" list!

The activities on pages 69–70 are from the *Junior Girl Scout Handbook*.

For more activities on decision-making, follow the Program Trail.

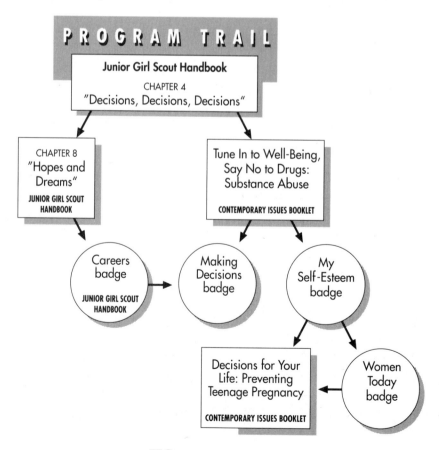

## PUTTING MY DECISION-MAKING SKILLS INTO PRACTICE

In a small group, share your experiences in making a difficult decision. What influenced your decision? What helped you decide? What was the result of your decision? What might you have done differently if you had had a second chance?

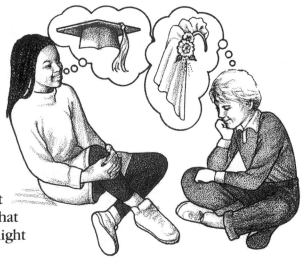

Make a list of the important decisions you will need to make in the next ten years. Some might be whether to go to college or whether to get a job, what kind of career to have, whether to get a car, when to get your own apartment, or whether or not to get married. Talk with at least three friends to find out about their plans for the future. Compare their plans with your own. How are their decisions similar to yours? different from yours? What are some decisions that women and girls make today that they might not have had to make in the past?

**1** _____

**2** _____

**3** _____

Think of the things and the people who influence your decisions. Some influences could be your family, your friends, your school, television, or a sports star you admire. Make a list of your influencers. Star (*) the people on this list whom you can approach when you need help in making a personal decision. What makes these people helpful? Think of different types of decisions. Are there certain people on your list whom you would go to for help with certain kinds of decisions? What makes them more helpful than others?

### *People Who Can Help Me*

**1** _____  **5** _____

**2** _____  **6** _____

**3** _____  **7** _____

**4** _____  **8** _____

71

Think of all the ways people try to pressure or force others into doing something they may not want to do. Some statements might be "Everybody's doing it," or "Try it—what are you afraid of?" Think of all the ways that you could answer those "pressure statements." "Well, I'm not everybody." "I don't need to do this to prove I am brave." Make a poster of typical "pressure statements" and answers you could give.

Talk about the following statements with your friends and classmates. What would you do if:

- A classmate offered you a cigarette on the way home from school.
- A group of friends stopped by to visit when no adults were home.
- You saw your sister take money from your father's wallet.
- Your cousin told you she was being abused by a relative and wanted you to promise to keep it a secret.
- Your family planned an outing on the same day as your best friend's birthday party.
- A bigger kid tried to bully you in the park.
- A stranger offered you money to sell some drugs.
- Some of your friends started teasing a classmate.

Try acting out the situations. What would be the best thing to do or say in each situation?

The activities on pages 71–72 are from the *Junior Girl Scout Handbook* and *Girl Scout Badges and Signs*.

For more activities on decision-making, follow the Program Trail.

PROGRAM TRAIL

Leadership badge
JUNIOR GIRL SCOUT HANDBOOK

My Community badge

Right to Read: Literacy
CONTEMPORARY ISSUES BOOKLET

My Self-Esteem badge

The World in My Community badge

Ready for Tomorrow badge

Making Decisions badge

Valuing Differences: Pluralism
CONTEMPORARY ISSUES BOOKLET

Earth Matters: A Challenge for Environmental Action
CONTEMPORARY ISSUES BOOKLET

# BEING A LEADER

Everyone has different strengths. Some people are very good at getting along with others. Some people always do well in school and never need to study. For some people, sports come easily. Others can organize people and get the job done. You will have many opportunities in life to use your special skills and talents to be a leader. You can be a leader by:

- Helping people to figure out what they want or need to do.
- Helping people to carry out the plans they have made.
- Encouraging people to make suggestions or to ask questions.
- Trying to help people cooperate with each other.
- Making someone feel more positive about herself and her abilities.

What do you think are the qualities of a leader? Write them here. Share the list with someone else. Are your lists the same? Which qualities are most important?

_____

_____

_____

_____

_____

Did you have any of these qualities on your list?

| | | |
|---|---|---|
| planning | accepting others | thinking clearly |
| directing | taking risks | working hard |
| being fair | advising | guiding |
| teaching | evaluating | sharing information |
| inspiring | showing enthusiasm | problem-solving |
| encouraging | organizing | respecting others |
| understanding others | cooperating | timekeeping |
| getting information | supporting | creating |

How could these qualities help the girls in this group?

The Super-Sleuth Detective Club was holding its monthly meeting. Vera, the club's president, called the meeting to order. Dianne, the club treasurer, reported that the club had $20 in its treasury and suggested that everyone discuss how to spend it. Judy said that was a good idea and that she would write the ideas on the chalkboard. Lisa came up with the first idea. "Let's buy a finger-printing kit and invisible ink. We could discover lots of clues and send secret messages!" Robyn, who had been quiet up until now, said, "That would use up all the

73

money! I'd rather save our club money and buy magnifying glasses for each of us! Spending all the money is stupid!" Judy said, "No way, Robyn, you shouldn't criticize other people's ideas, especially when yours aren't so great!" Robyn looked angry and said, "I was talking about Lisa's ideas, not yours!" Lisa asked Vera, "What do you think of my idea?" Vera answered, "I don't know. Let's vote on it."

Who took on leadership roles? Who is most similar to you?

Think of a time when you showed your leadership skills. What skills did you use? Write them here.

_____

_____

_____

_____

_____

The activities on pages 73–74 are from the *Junior Girl Scout Handbook*.

For more activities on leadership, follow the Program Trail.

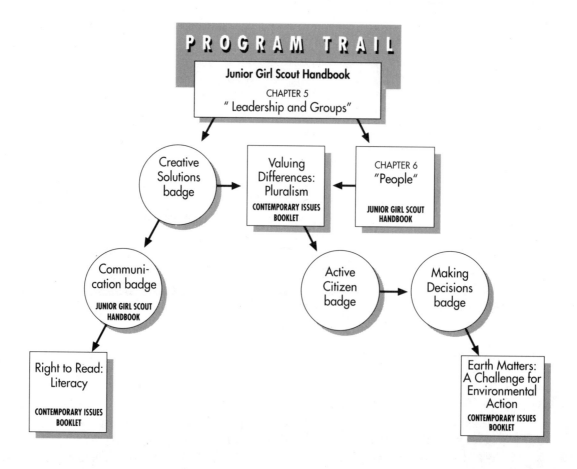

**T**here are many things that you can accomplish in a group that you cannot accomplish alone. However, working in a group can sometimes be hard if everyone has different ideas. That is when your leadership skills can be very helpful.

The steps that you use in planning activities are very similar to the steps that you use to make a decision.

## DRAW YOURSELF HERE!

### Step 1: Brainstorm Ideas

Share ideas and come up with new ones. Brainstorming is when everyone thinks of as many ideas as they can, no matter how crazy the ideas may sound. No one is allowed to criticize and all the ideas are written down. After a brainstorming session, the ideas are evaluated.

### Step 2: Make Decisions

You may find after brainstorming that you have too many good ideas. You could look over the ideas that the group has generated. Cut the list to those things that the group really wants to do. Combine similar ideas and eliminate ones that are impossible to do. Collect information about unfamiliar ideas. Discuss the good and bad points of each idea. Also, figure out if the ideas cost too much money or time to be practical. After considering all the ideas suggested, you can make final decisions about what you would like to do. You could vote on the ideas or have a general discussion. Remember that when deciding:

- Everyone should have a chance to speak.
- Only one person should talk at a time.
- Everyone should listen to the person who is talking, not interrupt or worry about what she wants to say next.
- Everyone should make her points quickly and not talk too long or too much.
- Everyone's comments should be considered.
- Only one topic at a time should be discussed.

### Step 3: Plan Your Calendar

### Step 4: Put Your Ideas into Action

It is important to know exactly what jobs need to be done and who will do them. People work better together when each person knows what is expected of her.

### Step 5: Evaluate What Was Done

Was it fun? Was it worthwhile? Could we have done some things differently? Would we do this again? Evaluation is an important part of planning. You know if you were successful. If you can't evaluate something, maybe you should not have done it in the first place.

With your friends or classmates, try this exercise in planning.

Your community has asked your group to help them clean up the environment. You will be given money and support from your local government. Your local newspaper would like to do a feature article on your efforts. The following are some environmental problems. You need to choose one and make a plan to solve it.

- Two downtown parks are being used as dumping sites for garbage and are full of weeds.
- Most commuters drive to work and do not carpool (only the driver is in the car, not a group). This causes pollution and congestion.
- The favorite stream for fishing has banks that are eroding and some trash being thrown into it.
- Your community recycles aluminum cans, but nothing else.
- Pick a real environmental problem in your community.

The activities on pages 75–76 are from the *Junior Girl Scout Handbook* and *Earth Matters: A Challenge for Environmental Action* Contemporary Issues booklet.

Look through the Girl Scout resources. What activities interest you? Try creating your own program trail.